FOLLOWING DHARMA

KATE HANSSEN

Following Dharma © 2023 Kate Hanssen. All Rights Reserved.

No part of this book may be reproduced in any form or by any electronic or mechanical means including information storage and retrieval systems, without permission in writing from the author. The only exception is by a reviewer, who may quote short excerpts in a review.

This is a work of non-fiction. The events and conversations in this book have been set down to the best of the author's ability, although some names and details may have been changed to protect the privacy of individuals. Every effort has been made to trace or contact all copyright holders. The publishers will be pleased to make good any omissions or rectify any mistakes brought to their attention at the earliest opportunity.

Printed in Australia

 A catalogue record for this work is available from the National Library of Australia

Subscribe today at http://www.reconnectiontours.com.au

Contents

Introduction... 2
Chapter 1: Unravelling................................. 12
Chapter 2: Heart Opening.............................. 17
Chapter 3: Deconstruction............................. 21
Chapter 4: To Follow Your Heart....................... 27
Chapter 5: Expansion and Contraction.................. 33
Chapter 6: I Do Believe In Fairy Tales, I Do, I Do.... 44
Chapter 7: Nurturing the Seeds........................ 51
Chapter 8: Yin and Yang............................... 54
Chapter 9: Fish Love.................................. 59
Chapter 10: Nepal 2013 – Letting Go and Falling In.... 64
Chapter 11: Kathmandu, Post Earthquake Day 4.......... 70
Chapter 12: Growing................................... 75
Chapter 13: Monsoon................................... 79
Chapter 14: Tiger Land................................ 89
Chapter 15: Culture, Language and Learning............ 95
Chapter 16: There Are Sometimes No Words............. 101
Chapter 17: Kali Doesn't Allow Maps.................. 103
Chapter 18 : Who's Your Guru?........................ 110
Chapter 19: False Evidence Appearing Real............ 115
Chapter 20: Shiva and Shakti......................... 119

Chapter 21: The Lotus. 128

Chapter 22: Community – A Tribal View 135

Chapter 23: Kali Kaleidoscope, We Are in Relationship With Everythin . .142

Chapter 24: Truth 147

Chapter 25: In the Darkness There is Always Light. 150

Chapter 26: Life is Long. 155

Chapter 27: Like a Bird. 160

Chapter 28: Teej, Celebrating the Goddess and Her God. 165

Chapter 29: Union. 169

Chapter 30: Bistaari. Bistaari, Just Breathe 174

Last Chapter 31: My Mother-In-Law Once Said To Me, 'Do they Have a Moon in Australia?'. 180

'Fortunately, some are born with spiritual immune systems that sooner or later give rejection to the illusory worldview grafted upon them from birth through social conditioning. They begin sensing that something is a-miss and start looking for answers. Inner knowledge and anomalous outer experiences show them a side to reality others are oblivious to, and so begins their journey of awakening. Each step of the journey is made by following the heart instead of following the crowd and by choosing knowledge over the veils of ignorance.'

HENRI BERGSON

Introduction

In my thirties I was reborn. Sounds like a cliched statement I know, however I cannot think of a better way to describe this time for me. I learnt how to crawl and walk again, in the sense that I was completely naïve and knew nothing about being an adult in the world.

I had been living in the role of wife and mother since I was seventeen years old. Some people would have thought I was too young to get married at twenty and raise a family, and perhaps I was. To say that, though, is to negate the very experiences that helped shape who I am now, so I choose to integrate all of it. I am not that much into regrets or 'what ifs' and at around the age of twenty-eight, things started to change. I was rediscovering a curiosity and innocence that was with me as a child. I was in awe, simultaneously scared, excited about the possibilities and opportunities that lay ahead.

It was during this time I discovered my multi-dimensionality. I learnt I am many things and, like the universe that holds us, I am continuously expanding, contracting, growing and changing. Forever a traveller and explorer of both the inner and outer worlds, creator, writer, mother, singer, dancer, guitarist, guidance counsellor, facilitator, speaker, teacher, goddess, healer, intuitive, abundant and ever-evolving being. I'd been gathering new tools for my bucket for as long as I could remember and now I was learning what 'my dharma' was, although I did not know it at the time.

Awareness

I learnt that reconnection is a choice. After years of emotional turmoil, suffering, guilt and accumulated negativity, I felt like giving up. Throughout my marriage, I often felt like a lost cause. The marriage certainly was. I'd pondered if I even deserved anything greater or not. Should I just settle for my reality despite its oppression, negativity, and challenges? Sometimes it all just got too much, and I found myself in the pit of despair, thinking I was not even worthy of having these thoughts or feelings at all. I felt selfish and worthless. I was, no doubt, suffering from the modern disease of 'I am not enough'. However, I am now aware of the slow decaying of the soul caused by what is commonly recognised as emotional abuse and gaslighting.

To choose life on this planet is to choose all the experiences, perceived positive and negative. We cannot live on planet earth, a planet of duality, and not experience duality. Yet we are all trying to avoid it and take the easy way, always looking for the path of least resistance. Which, in fact, becomes the path of suffering, numbness and disease. A big call I know, but I believe it wholeheartedly and here is why; for us to evolve, grow and learn, we need to experience all the forces, negative and positive. The shadow is where our greatest truths, knowledge, and wisdom come from.

To be balanced beings, to shift and grow, we need to recognise that love exists in both the dark and the light. Otherwise, we would all still be cave men and rubbing stones together to make our fires. Not everything that exists can be beautiful, perfect, and divine all the time. The energy here on this planet can be challenging in this way. However, I believe it is created perfectly for maximum growth and evolution to happen.

The universe can be all things as are we. A peaceful/equally chaotic, imperfect/perfect place. Just like the seasons of the year.

To reconnect is to forgive ourselves, to forgive others, to live in the present and to know our place, to really feel, taste, touch and experience.

It is to accept the NOW and recognise that all power and opportunity exist in the present moment. From this space of connection, we can grow, evolve, and change our reality by changing the way we perceive, what we believe, and therefore what we choose. It is important to understand that everything has a role to play, everything has been created by us, for us, in co-creation with universal law, the real 'truth'.

Happiness

There seems to be a happiness addiction, an idea that we all need to strive for happiness and be happy all the time. We take pills to maintain a sense of balance and to avoid slipping into the dark. This has become the norm in our society, the pursuit of happiness. The sad part is that it is only half of you. It is not the whole of you. You cannot evolve, learn or grow without the pain and challenges, they are perfectly created to push you to grow.

Have you ever noticed that we always remember the bad experiences over the good? We are designed that way.

How you experience these challenges, though, is where the choice is. We cannot avoid them, and the more we try, the more negativity and suffering we will create. Resistance creates suffering, stagnancy and a slow death. Life is about flow. Think about it in terms of the weather or a river. Seasons always cycle, they never stop, and the river always flows. If it is blocked it either overflows and floods, but keeps moving, or the water can stagnate and become blocked resulting in it eventually drying up. The planet may seem chaotic sometimes, with earthquakes, fires, floods, volcanoes, tsunamis; but she will always balance herself, no matter what.

Through the chaos, she is often transformed; always deconstructing, creating, changing, moving, expanding, and contracting. She never stops. We are truly just micro versions of her. I often wondered if I had been asleep all those years between childhood and turning twenty-eight or wrapped in a type of bubble wrap; just bouncing from one experience to another without really being present or actually feeling it. Was it possible I hadn't really touched the ground in my life? I felt I had experienced most of my life up to that point, floating above it, distanced and disconnected.

I guess this helped me feel safe. I will boldly say that many of us are not grounded at all; in that we are not connected or able to feel life in its truest form. I think as humans we avoid pain of all kinds and because of this, we often don't experience genuine joy and happiness either. Hence the endless seeking for the next temporary high.

In Indonesia and other similar cultures, there are ceremonies that celebrate the moment that a baby's soul touches the earth for the first time. Before this ceremony, the child is carried everywhere and never put on the ground. If the child is put down too soon, it is believed the soul does not integrate fully, creating a split in the child's psyche and potentially setting them up for a very disconnected life. In modern medicine, this manifests as disorders such as psychosis or bipolar. In these cultures, there are shamans (natural medicine people) that help in these situations. The people seek counsel from them to help the souls fully integrate and heal their suffering.

Govinda, my second husband, is Nepalese. He has witnessed many occasions of a shaman at work with people in his society; people who had been labelled 'mad' or completely disconnected from the community. The shaman would assist them in integrating and reconnecting their soul with their body. He explained these people had usually been ostracised or unable to contribute to society and were taken to the shaman for healing.

After studying at the transpersonal art therapy school in Melbourne, I believe this is definitely an area we should look to learn more about. My lecturer, who was previously an anthropologist lecturer at La Trobe University, shared extensive studies and reports with us. It seems more is being done in this field relating to shamans and healing mental health issues.

Empathy – (Don't absorb, just observe)

To empathise with something or someone is to have compassion and understanding. It is to perceive or feel the energy of the person or thing you tune into – choosing to experience their pain, their suffering, and equally, their happiness. However, it seems we find it easier to empathise with pain than joy.

An empathic, intuitive person is known as clairsentient; they can empathically feel what another person or being is experiencing. It can be both a gift of serving others and excruciatingly painful.

I urge anyone who feels they might be an empath to learn how to manage this energy to help discern what is yours and what is not; and particularly the art of learning to let go. You can learn to do it. I believe it is something all humans need to embody and master to make the world a more peaceful and loving place. The fact is, we can all be clairsentient if we practice.

The energy of empathy is very different from sympathy. Empathy is a positive energy that allows for expansion, learning, and love. Sympathy is negative and contracting. It distorts the experience or tries to divert it, oppressing or enabling the negative energy to remain and keep playing out, a bit like a broken record.

When we empathise with someone, we are allowing them the space to experience their journey with support through the darkness; we are walking beside them, not doing the work for them, and certainly not denying them or protecting them from the experience.

Everyone and everything on the planet is responsible for their own growth and the relationships they have with everything around them. When we empathise with others, animals, plants and the earth, we are becoming more in tune with the needs, desires, values and energies that are all around us; we are more conscious about our actions. We recognise we are connected through invisible threads and we understand we can only love. We expand, we evolve and we allow others to evolve through their experiences as well. We are not in judgment. We are acknowledging the challenges and unique experiences of every soul and not judging them. Through empathy, we can heal ourselves and others, by sharing the understanding of a common journey we all face, life, growth, change or birth, life and death.

A survival technique of empaths is to become observers and avoiders of suffering, feeling through the pain of others, instead of feeling their own. I know this is true for me and many people I have worked with over the years.

In my counselling and mentoring programs, I would often work with people who were trying to navigate life as empaths. I noticed a common thread between their issues and their inability to be grounded, and they were often disconnected. It is well documented that many psychologists or behavioural therapists are drawn to the helping fields to understand their own pain; they are learning about it through other people's experiences. Empathy can be difficult for a sensitive person. Sometimes, they can be too empathic, not being able to differentiate between their own suffering and somebody else's. Empaths feel the pain of others as their own.

I learnt I was an empath; I felt too much and took everything personally. Over the years, I disconnected from life, becoming an observer. I was not truly experiencing anything, rather feeling through others. Watching from afar, judging and trying to maintain a safe distance. I now know that this is a common theme for many of us as a way of protecting ourselves against the perceived pain and suffering that exists in the world. We are often quite sensitive and avoid feeling our own pain.

For a long time, I felt like I had been asleep, unconscious. I remember the moment I stirred from my slumber. When I was about twenty-four, I turned my head to look at the three children sitting in the back seat of my car. I had the sudden realisation that they were real and I really was a mother of three young boys.

This might sound strange to you, you may even think I'm a little bonkers. However, I have had many moments in my life I would call 'aha' moments, where all the cogs in the wheel simply slot into place, or out of place, as the case may be. Then I am shocked at feeling or experiencing what it is to be human on this planet. This honestly jolted me into my reality as three wide-eyed boys stared back at me, as if we'd met for the first time! I was responsible for these lives until they could be responsible for their own lives. I really did not feel equipped to do that, as I had no idea what life was about.

I had always been aware of what I call a universal/global awareness; I was aware people suffered, animals suffered. In many of the self-help courses I'd participated in, they never taught me how to live with both the dark and light, the connection, and the disconnection. It was not complete.

I honestly think that without direct experience and the willingness to reflect and learn, then no course will really assist you to become 'whole'. There has to be a willingness to go on the pilgrimage, to go on the journey and experience it all in equal measure – the challenges, opportunities, ups and downs, and ultimately the blessings, synchronicities and joys. To learn with nature, our true teacher, of all that life is. To watch the marathon does not give the same feeling or integrated learning experience as does running it. How could I say I know about marathons if I had never run one? To truly know, I would have to run each step of the journey.

I realised the fraudulent feelings I was having was because I was not experiencing anything myself. It is the very reason we are here on this planet, to have the experience.

Over thousands of years, the biggest lessons and breakthroughs in evolution have come through experiential living. Through modern lifestyles, we have found ourselves disconnected. We sit in classrooms, go to jobs and most of our learning comes from books, screens, and authorities. We learn to recite, regurgitate and form opinions based on other people's perceptions and views. Is it any wonder we lack faith and have anxiety, self-doubt, and procrastination?

I had to learn from my experience. Without it, I could not be grounded, connected and confident to trust in my ability to handle my potential power or creation. Robotic living never worked for me. I had this habit of upending the pot when things became a little boring and routine. Which was fine until one day something destroyed my reality completely. My core beliefs were left so rattled that it left me lying amid rubble and destruction, having to rebuild myself one brick at a time.

When we are in balance, we are connected to both source and self. Disconnection comes when we resist the feeling, when we avoid the situation, when we (our ego) don't want to see the reality. It is common in times of trauma, stress, disease and other trials of human life that we can disconnect. It's a natural defence mechanism of the ego to keep us safe.

Separation

The day I chose to leave my first husband was both a day of relief and liberation; yet it meant the loss of what I thought was love, stability, security and a big part of what had become my identity. In short, my whole belief system was about to be completely upended.

Seventeen years is a long time to be with one person and at thirty-four, I guess it was half of my life, the other half being a child with my parents. Leaving home at seventeen to move to Western Australia, over 3,000 kilometres away from all that was familiar, I was excited about the adventure. I never once considered if I'd miss anyone or worried about any of the negatives. At heart, I was always a traveller and explorer, even as a child. Looking back, it was the best thing I ever did to get out into the world and challenge my perceptions. However, it meant the beginning of a life where I became dependent on a man who almost certainly had a onedimensional view of what the future was.

In those days, things were simpler. I felt I was mature enough and knew what I had to do; get a job, get a man, get married and raise kids, not necessarily in that order, although that is what I did. I mean, that's what every woman in my family did, and mostly, growing up in the Yarra Valley in Victoria, it was what most people did. This was 'normal'. Well, at least that was what was being mirrored to me in my small portion of the world.

Who knew this would not be enough to satisfy my soul? That fourteen years after saying 'I do', my restlessness and the feeling of walls caving in on me would send a series of waves rippling out to divide me and my first husband. It seemed my soul had its own journey and mission and it would not be tamed, no matter how hard I tried to work with it. It wanted growth! I felt like I had two people living inside me. The lion and the mouse.

By the age of thirty-one, I'd had four beautiful children, three biological boys and one daughter adopted from Ethiopia. It doesn't need much imagination to understand the decision to leave was not an easy one. I wrestled with leaving for at least seven years, a soft remote voice often gently asking me to look at my life and our compatibility.

If I am truly honest with myself now, I never saw a future for us. We were too different, our values were miles apart, and I was just too young and too scared to voice mine. On the surface, I had everything a modern family could want. I had a hard-working husband who was committed to his career and financially supportive. I had a beautiful home at the foot of the Dandenong Ranges with cows, chooks, and a bungalow to work from. I should have been grateful, right?

Yet our marriage lacked depth, it lacked connection; it was mundane, routine, without spark. There was no passion. Looking back, it had no mutual respect or reverence and we, as people, had come to mirror this.

Intuitively, I knew my first husband had been unfaithful and although I had no proof at this stage; I felt it was inevitable the way things were between us. We could not have been more different. I had lost every part of who I thought I was and I was a far cry from the curious, excitable, busy and ambitious child I had been. We were so far apart from each other living this modern lifestyle. The more I worked on myself and tried to reconnect, the further he disconnected and the more alienated and alone I felt in our marriage.

Despite the nightmares about him leaving me and the affairs he was having, we had both convinced ourselves we could stay in this for the kids. I was so naïve, not once questioning the sudden urgency two years before we separated, when he had me signing all sorts of documents. He was busy creating family trusts and other accounting documents that were supposedly about setting things up the best way for our finances. Later, it became clear he was preparing for the inevitable. I guess he knew it was just a matter of time before I found out about the affairs and left him.

I had lived and experienced many things in my life very fast. It seems, despite my perception of myself, I was a fast learner and on a fast track of growth. For most of my adult life, I had felt like I was an observer, never feeling like a co-creator at all. When I think about this, I see now that I was numb, fearful, and just scared to step into my power and to truly connect. I think I believed the connection would be painful. I was going through the motions of life, disconnected, avoiding pain and suffering in this limbo state. I was shutting down more each day from everyone and everything; to avoid feeling the hurt that was being created by my relationship and my outdated belief system. I needed to grow up.

I became a helper to distract myself, a diploma in counselling to legitimise it.

Finally, I'd had enough after a fight over money, a measly $35. It was just the excuse he needed, and I gave up trying. This chapter had come to an end.

It was time to step into and onto the earth in its entirety and this was exactly what my soul/self was craving. I needed to immerse myself, get in the water to really understand how to swim.

Living on planet earth and trying to avoid any negativity, pain and suffering is like experiencing the daytime only. How tiring. Imagine this life with no moonlight, no dark night, no stars. How do we fully understand love and compassion if we have not experienced being vulnerable and rejected? There is love in the dark too – love of self and soul.

My safe and secure life was a false reality, full of pretending and living on the surface. It was disconnected from anything real and certainly had no acknowledgement of the shadow. This imbalance was keeping me from my dharma.

I was numb; I was slowly dying inside, lacking any motivation or enthusiasm or purpose. It was time to feel, touch, taste, see, hear, and know the world. I had been born to experience life, not just skirt around the edges, playing it safe.

> *'Sometimes letting things go is an act of far greater power than defending or hanging on.'*
>
> ECKHART TOLLE

Chapter 1
Unravelling

After I separated from my first husband, I started getting better at being alone. I slowly explored my creative side, through encouragement from some self-help books I'd been reading at the time. Louise Hay's 'Heal Your Life' and Wayne Dyer's 'Intention' had been my buddies for some time, along with Dan Millman's 'The Life You Were Born to Live'. This was thanks in part to a beautiful psychotherapist I had met who literally changed my life and helped me get at least one foot on the ground. Through her, I learnt about meditation, consciousness, and psychic awareness, and to trust my intuition.

My absolute favourite books, then and now, were Paulo Coelho's novels, which I've journeyed with many times. They always seemed to find their way into my hands when I was travelling somewhere and, notably, always shared the exact message I needed to receive at the time. I think it was Paulo's and OSHO's books that had the biggest impact on me; asking me to step into life in a more conscious way, to be courageous, vulnerable and brave. They really highlighted for me the shadow work and the understanding of experiential learning and integration. When reading Paulo, I felt like I was journeying with him; I felt like I understood the pilgrim's journey, as I too, was a pilgrim. I think my inspiration for writing and sharing my story, in the hope it will help someone else, came from him.

However, the book I was reading on our last family holiday together before the separation resonated with me. Elizabeth Gilbert's 'Eat Pray

Love' gave me the understanding of what I was seeking; connection, purpose, and the depth of a love that created an expansion of the heart.

After I left my ex-husband, I experienced many 'firsts'. I was in my thirties and felt I had not had a 'rite of passage'. I guess I missed out on that, being a young mother, and now, here I was with the chance to do my teen years and twenties all over again.

There was my first music festival, my first drunk night out alone, my first joint, my first sexual relationship other than my ex-husband, my first overseas trip alone, buying my first house alone, my first walk of shame, my first road trip, my first open mic session, my first concert, and the list goes on...

I met so many amazing, wonderful characters who brought to life stories and parts of myself that lay dormant, like seeds waiting for the sun to shine upon them. Like the cliched butterfly metamorphosis, I morphed, transformed, changed, broke down, deconstructed, and reconstructed. It did not stop.

There were so many 'normals' and it brought me to this place of reinventing myself the way I wanted to be, instead of being a rolling stone at the mercy of the bumps and knocks. It was up to me to create me, and I loved the creating part.

Often people around me struggled with the changes they witnessed and at times, I felt judged, alone and caged. So many of these feelings about me were, in fact, my own fear. Fear of being judged and rejected or ostracised by the tribe. The strange or perhaps truthful part was, I never felt part of the tribe anyway. It was never a fit for me. It always felt too small and restricted and to be a part of it, I had to play small. I no longer wanted to play that role in this community. I wanted to find my own tribe. I needed to connect.

The more I listened to my soul, my creativity and intuition, the more I was able to step fearlessly out of the mundane, the safe haven; and every time I left my comfort zone, I grew.

I know now that I am not alone and that many people I have met have experienced so many things, yet this does not always define who they are. I love that two of my dearest friends, each twenty years older than me, had so much wisdom to share. They shared with me openly and showed me it was my rite of passage to explore this world with every ounce of enthusiasm and in every aspect. To sail the widest stretches, trek mountains and sleep in a stranger's bed were all legit experiences and could never be judged; because when we choose to act on something in the moment, we usually choose what we want to experience.

It was important to be conscious at least and take responsibility for that. Everything that I felt the desire or needed to know about being human on planet earth was there to be experienced if I chose, not judged or limited. Earth is a playground in which to explore and learn. This amazing ability we all have to create and be a part of creation is within us all.

So just prior to my fortieth birthday and after an emotional court battle with the ex-husband, I was exhausted and drained. It was here that I had a revelation and a harsh realisation that in order to move on completely, I had to let go. Let go of everything. I faced my deepest fears and looked at myself honestly. I saw how much my misery, depression and toxic connection to the ex-husband was hindering my abilities to be a good mother and human in general.

I was not in any state to be the person I wanted to be. Despite fighting so hard for my daughter and winning the case, for my soul, for my heart and for her too, I needed to let go.

I could not endure any more fighting. I had tried multiple times in different ways to connect and create an amicable relationship for the children. I could not understand my ex-husband's actions and behaviour and no matter how much I may have been able to have a friendship with him, perhaps he just could not.

The lawyers, as they do, loved the case; they saw lots of dollar signs (at least seven of them). My lawyer's advice was to pursue and get what I deserved as the mother of four children. However, I realised the mental health of their father, me and the kids was more important. So, I took a payout to end the case.

I was exhausted emotionally and did not understand why this had all happened. It was later I dropped my bundle. I could not fight anymore. I had nothing left in the tank. The extra money gave me an opportunity to take a break from life… So I took it. I let go of everything.

It was his turn; the children needed to know him, the real him. I had to stop protecting them from their reality, from the reality of him. They deserved the truth, as I did. I had always been there and sacrificed for them. I could give them no more and in trying to, I was constantly running ragged, which meant they did not get the best version of me. If I wasn't able to follow my heart, how could they? I owed them the truth of who we both are, their father and me. No longer could I live a lie, trying to be something that I was not. It was imperfectly perfect; the universe had provided me with what I had been asking for and I had never seen it until this moment.

I had the perfect youthful parents who were active and present in my children's lives and lived in a stable domestic environment. I had an ex-husband who did the same. He earnt plenty of money, had a good (new) wife and a big house, and he also desired to have his children with him. Despite our differences, he wanted the best for his children. For the first time, the timing was perfect.

The following weeks brought about one of the hardest decisions I had ever made. In the days after sending my daughter to live with her father, I cried in the bathtub and considered ending my life. I considered many things and was judging myself very harshly as a failure as a wife, mother and, fundamentally, as a human.

I was certain everyone around me thought I'd lost my mind. In a sense I had. I had listened to my heart, and this was one of the first times I noticed that listening to the heart required bravery and courage. I was in this moment cracked and broken apart. Vulnerable.

After a few days, my son reminded me he was going to Nepal for a trekking holiday. I immediately felt the pull to revisit Nepal. As soon as I had that thought, he suggested I go with him. Not knowing what the universe had in store for me and with nothing holding me back anymore and nothing more to lose, I booked my ticket.

I was in Nepal on 25 April when the 7.8 earthquake brought the country to rubble, and as it deconstructed, so did I.

Chapter 2
Heart Opening

We met Govin at the airport and as soon as I saw him, all the feelings came rushing back. You see, I met him for the first time back in 2013. I was guided to come to Nepal then too; my cousin had suggested it after I had broken up with my first husband a second time.

Nepal had certainly stolen a piece of my heart. It has an energy I cannot describe, and I found myself trekking in the Himalayas with my youngest son.

I felt an undeniable connection between two souls as soon as Govin and I made eye contact, and here it was, two years later, and the strangest feelings re-emerged. I knew the first time we met there was something special about him. When I left after that three-week holiday, I vowed to return. Although that feeling had escaped me until I returned and looked into his eyes again in 2015.

The first time we met in 2013, he was so young and I was still grieving many things about the loss of my marriage and previous life. I did not allow myself to consider him as a lover. But I could not understand the feelings I had. They were so foreign to me, like nothing I had ever known before. There was a familiarity about him. It did not make sense. I dismissed the feelings that surfaced about him because of his age, and to be honest, I was not ready for love at that time. Nor was my heart open to receive anything unconditionally without judgment.

So here I was once more on Nepal soil and this time it was 2015. Arriving back in Pokhara, a gorgeous lakeside at the base of the Annapurnas. I was confused about how I was feeling and decided in the moment to just go with it and not judge it. Maybe it was just the feeling of connection after a harrowing eighteen months, but something else told me it was more than that and to stay open, so I did.

Within a few days, my son went trekking with him and I decided to focus on healing activities. I had got sick on the journey over, so sick that I ended up doing nothing for the first few days. I did some meditation with Baba G, a funny yogi dude who is a conundrum of sorts and, by Australian standards, probably completely mad. However, I found him a welcome distraction and a light-hearted soul at a time when I needed it. I did a little yoga and immersed myself in the Nepali culture.

Govin and my son were away trekking. It was so strange; I missed Govin so much, I could not understand the feeling, it was like a grief. I still did not really know him, although something in me felt like I knew him better than anyone. It was weird. Like nothing I'd experienced before, so I vowed once again to not judge and be open.

It took a while for my health to come good and I decided it was just great to be in Pokhara, writing, relaxing, meditating, walking and exploring Nepali life. I focused on the culture and learnt about Nepal. During the next three weeks, I went to a Nepali wedding, visited villages, explored Nepalese life, and I genuinely started to relax.

When Govin and my son returned, Govin invited us to his home in Baglung. This was common in Nepal, as most of the locals loved to take foreigners to visit their homes. We, of course, accepted the invite and took the four-hour taxi ride to Baglung.

Baglung was beautiful. It felt so natural. I felt so connected to the Nepali people and especially Baglung village, that I can honestly only describe it as a familiar feeling of coming home. It was so strange and as I was so open; I was experiencing this visit in a way that told me this would not be the last time I visited. Something about Baglung was oddly familiar and comfortable. I felt I could just set up a little home there and live. This was one week before the earthquake in Nepal.

Still, to this day, the most memorable moments were sharing with him – his family, his village, the music, and many conversations. Although sometimes challenging due language barriers, somehow, I felt we understood each other; it was truly amazing. I really felt connected to something deeper, a knowing, almost like I was being divinely guided to be a part of his world and him mine. It was like we had some divine gifts for each other; and even if the humanness in us was not aware of what they were, some part of us knew we were exchanging something meaningful.

Whilst visiting Baglung, we went for a lovely walk and Govin pointed out the Kali River. I recalled my small amount of knowledge on the goddess Kali (a Hindu goddess) and remembered she was the goddess of destruction and creation. I had meditated with Kali and asked for her guidance as I moved through destructive periods of my life. I had asked her to guide me in the dark moments so I could find my way to the light and start creating again.

I even brought the Kali necklace with me to Nepal on this trip. Whilst packing, I came across the necklace, which my girlfriend had gifted me a long time ago, and it ignited my interest in the goddess. Why it had popped up at that moment, just as I was about to head to Nepal, was a mystery to me.

In the past six to eight years, I had been deconstructing and recreating regularly and felt quite an affinity with Kali. Like being reunited with an old friend in the land in which she was born, through thousands of years of ritual, culture and religion.

I became aware at once of her presence in this Baglung Village, with the amazing Kali Gandaki River beneath us. It rushed by, carrying the ashes of the dead that were regularly burnt on its shores in Hindu funeral ceremonies. I also felt the presence in the Kali temple that stood high on the bluff above the river.

I felt it quite fitting to be there, especially after the long destructive cycle with my ex-husband. I was ready to recreate a new chapter of my life. Little did I know that this was also the prequel to the next life-changing events about to unfold. I think it was in this moment I decided I was ready to create again and invite love back into my l life.

A few weeks later my son was returning home to Australia, and we wanted to help our friend Govin (I had not yet shared my feelings with him) come to Australia in the future. Govin had expressed a number of times that his dream was to go to Australia to change his life, and we wanted to help him somehow realise this dream.

I still had another week in Nepal. We had visited his home and seen the hardships of Nepali life and we could not get past the generosity of the Nepali people. Govin had devoted himself to us and looked after us whilst we were there, even though his father was in intensive care in hospital, after a long thirty years of alcohol abuse. I would learn more about this story later.

Nepalis are renowned for their humble and giving personality. They look after guests like family and actually hold them in the highest regard, taking this responsibility seriously. Forever grateful, we wanted to give back in some way. We could at least help him get a passport and promised him we would help him to come to Australia in whatever way we could. I was thinking maybe that was my purpose here.

'Creation and Destruction are one, to the eyes that can see Beauty'

SAVITRI DEVI

Chapter 3
Deconstruction

On 25 April, 2015, I was sitting in a cafe in Thamel, a touristy area of Kathmandu, the capital city of Nepal. The Olive Tree café was a favourite of mine as it was hidden behind walls that allowed you to get some solitude away from bustling Thamel.

Thamel, a touristy suburb of Kathmandu, could be a fullon experience that was chaotic and intense. Kathmandu is an amazing kaleidoscope of smells, sounds, tastes, and experiences that have all your senses alive and buzzing. For an empath like me, that could be overwhelming, but equally inspiring and wondrous.

At the café, I sipped a banana Lassi, a combination of milk, yoghurt and fruit, which I can honestly say is unique to this part of the world. I've tried to replicate it many times and yet it never tastes the same as it does in Nepal. Govin tells me it is because the bananas are different, organic.

The next minute, my table started to shake. The floor and everything that was fixed seemed to become liquid and vibrate. Within seconds, I was hanging on to the large concrete pillar next to me, watching people running from the upstairs rooms to the floor, and chaos ensued. People started to run everywhere, yelling and screaming. Things were falling from walls and glasses smashed on to the bricked floor. We were all holding onto solid structures and standing in doorways, despite the fact we still had not fully realised what we were experiencing. It seemed we had the intuition to go to the strongest part of the building.

After about forty seconds (it seemed like five minutes), I realised it was an earthquake. It was the strangest sensation, almost like standing on a raft, on rough water, with no way to balance yourself. Not being familiar with earthquakes, I had no idea how destructive it had been, and I could not see outside.

After what seemed like ten minutes, I noticed everyone just standing around looking bewildered. Then slowly the chatter started and for a moment, everything just stopped. It was soon obvious that nobody knew what to do, and then the noise of the street outside became louder. A whole new level of chaos was erupting outside, as Nepali people and tourists were running everywhere and shops were slamming their doors shut. I asked the Nepali staff what to do, and they shrugged.

'We never have like this before', they said. It was clear everyone was in shock and uncertain of what to do.

I remembered from the recesses of my mind that in earthquakes you want to be away from buildings, so I decided my first action would be to get out of Thamel, and quickly. Thamel is old and many of the buildings are storeys high, without modern standards in building codes. They are certainly not the safest buildings. Even without an earthquake, they often look in high need of maintenance.

The streets are very narrow in Thamel, which made it challenging to find open space. I calculated the distance back to my guesthouse (maybe one thousand metres) and figured I had maybe a few minutes before the aftershocks came.

I walked back briskly, all the time looking up. I noticed some walls down and people crying. However, I was not really taking it in. I was most likely in shock and in flight or fight mode, with a clear focus on what I needed to do to get safe. I felt strongly that I really needed to get to safety first and then assess the damage and what to do. The streets were even more crazy than usual and people were running in many directions, all doing the same thing, trying to find safety away from the potential collapse of buildings. It was difficult to take it all in. Actually, much later we learnt that most of the damage and casualties came from the aftershocks than the earthquake itself.

I arrived back at the guest house I'd been staying in to find more shocked and confused people, and soon it was apparent this was not a Nepali experience. This was something very different. The power was gone, no phones, no Wi-Fi.

We were in the dark for forty-eight hours before we learnt the magnitude of the quake. Many tourists were overwhelmed with grief and emotions running wild. Most of them headed as quickly as possible to their embassies to leave Nepal as soon as possible.

At this point, I was not aware of the size and damage to Nepal and did not think Australians would have heard about the event. The earthquake killed 9,000 people and injured nearly 22,000. It was 7.8 on the Richter scale. The only reason there were not more casualties was because Nepal was an under-developed country. Many people were working on the farms or outside at that time of day.

My new friends at the guest house set up a radio, and we started to find out information over the radio, which my Nepali friends would translate. It was only then I thought about the news reaching Australia, and no doubt my family was fearing for my safety. I tried multiple times to contact them, but all the lines were down.

It was probably at this point the magnitude of it all sank in. The possibility that I could have been injured, or worse still, dead in a foreign country, was a reality. It was in this moment, despite concern about my family's worry, that I found a quiet resolve… I was alive, still breathing, so were many others and that it was okay. It was a funny feeling, almost a calmness that came over me, that I was being guided and was completely safe.

Many tourists arrived looking for safety and food. We would help them by sharing our food and helping with directions to the embassy. However, after two days it was getting harder to source food and water, as all stores were shut. Kathmandu had come to a halt. It was feeling like a ghost town. Many Nepali had rushed to their villages to help their families. Later, I learned of the damage and loss throughout Nepal, which helped shape my part in this experience. Somehow, I was part of this divine creation or destruction.

On the third night after the quake, we had nine packets of two-minute noodles to feed twenty-five people. Over the past few days, word had spread amongst the tourists that we were the goto place for that area of Thamel. A little area known as Paknajol. We'd become a drop-in place for tourists to come to for support. Some of them had no idea what to do, some of them as young as eighteen.

I had become part of the Nepali crew supporting the tourists, and in some respects, acting as their interpreter or advocate. Despite my external calmness and ability to support the tourists, I was becoming aware of the difficulty in getting resources.

I recall trying to get word to my family in Oz to tell them I was okay, as I knew by now the news would have been all over the event; no doubt exaggerating everything, creating fear and panic in my family back home. The other person who would not leave my mind was Govinda. Was he okay? Was his family okay? All my friends in Pokhara, were they okay? Pokhara was an eight-hour bus ride away and without power, we had no way of contacting anyone.

People were showing signs of post-traumatic stress syndrome and sleeping outside had become the norm. This was the safest place to be up till now, as the aftershocks were causing more damage than the actual quake and were sometimes even stronger.

To distract ourselves, we'd play guitar, mingle with each other, talk about home and play cards. It was an eerie feeling, but just before every shock, I recall a strange earthly calm, like the vibration of the earth stopping, like a motor stalling. Then the birds would start flying and chirping and the dogs would start barking, and sure enough, the next tremor would take place, creating more panic and fear.

The tremors would come often over the next few weeks. Those first five days were harrowing, and most people slept outside or not at all, with their shoes on and bags packed, ready to run. Quite a few of the hotels and larger multi-floor buildings were not safe to enter, so Kathmandu had become a sea of blue and orange tarps. Thankfully, this time of year was pretty warm, so being outside wasn't too bad.

By day four, I really needed to think about what to do next. It finally hit me the magnitude of this thing, and I needed to think about my own safety. For a moment, I had got quite caught up in looking after others, as this was my natural state; however, I realised this, in part, could be my own post-traumatic stress in action.

I finally got a message out to Australia via Facebook, and the flood of messages that came back was somewhat amazing. Actually, it was these messages that jolted me into reality. Until that point, it had all seemed like a bit of a dream that was happening to everyone else. I had not even thought about the fact that it was happening to me too. I had never contemplated how many people cared or I might miss me if I was gone. It was a strange feeling. Almost like I imagine, being at your own funeral, and seeing people you had not thought about for a long time show up and express their grief.

Govin finally got through to me and said he was coming to Kathmandu. He and his family were fine. Baglung sits high on a large rock that was not really affected by the quake. He was laughing and somewhat at ease once he'd found out I was okay.

The bus to Kathmandu from Baglung would be over twelve hours long and I told him not to take the journey, as it might be dangerous and we did not know what impacts the quake may have had in other areas along the way. He was determined and somehow, Govin made it to Kathmandu the next day. I cried when I saw him. He was okay, and in typical Nepali fashion, he was almost laughing about the madness of it all, saying, 'ke garne, Nepali jindagi', what to do...Nepali life.

He tried to convince me to go home to Australia, however, I explained to him from the moment the earthquake happened, I did not feel any inclination to go home. I only felt more determined to stay. Something was guiding me strongly and my heart was begging me to stay and help. I felt I owed Nepal that, as it had been so good to me.

Govin relented and suggested that I should go to Pokhara by air. Despite my reservations, in the end I agreed, thinking it would be safer than the roads. He reported the roads were a mess, and it was crazy driving on them. Even he, as a local, had no idea what to expect. In the end, I guess being in the air was better than being on the ground in an earthquake.

It is funny, but at no stage did I feel the need to go home to Australia. In every part of my being, I felt I was where I was supposed to be. The clarity and calm that had found me in those few days amidst the chaos was surreal. Looking back, I see I had been catapulted through extreme circumstances into my heart space. I felt more vulnerable, courageous and grounded than ever. I was without fear for the first time. It was almost like the universe had said, 'you have something bigger to do, it is not your time yet'. I'd been jolted into the very present!

'The supreme secret of the inner journey is the path of love. If we can possess our whole heart with contemplation of the beloved, we will experience the wonders and beauty of the universe.'

RUMI

Chapter 4
To Follow Your Heart

How often in our modern lives do we hear the words 'from the heart' or 'follow your heart'? How many of us have ever stopped to consider exactly what these words really mean?

The past had definitely taught me a few things about following the heart. It was during my time in Nepal that I began to understand more about what that really looks like and feels like. Following one's heart was not necessarily going to rid me of the fear I was perceiving around me; it often accelerated it.

When I turned and faced what I was fearing and took action, this was my heart in action, the true meaning of activism. A heart in action requires 'courage', the thought of that immediately reminding me of the lion in the 'Wizard of Oz' and his desire for courage. In the past, I often misunderstood this energy as anxiety and then misused this energy, which created the symptoms I now know to be soul excitement. If you recall, the lion did seem rather anxious, until he realised courage was in him all along.

I have found that anxiety is the unchannelled energy of nervous excitement of imminent change or uncertainty. In fact, it is the soul getting excited about challenge and growth. Our soul knows that it is here to be challenged and grow. Its whole purpose is to learn. However, because of society's habit of trying to control and maintain the status quo, we create a misdirection of energy. Therefore, we experience this energy as anxiety and not excitement and readiness for change.

I realised that to follow my heart, I needed to make friends with anxiety, reframe it and use it. I started to recognise and learn the language of my soul. Some might call this intuition. I started understanding the needs of it and eventually understood what it was to follow my dharma, my purpose; always expanding and contracting, forever moving, changing and growing in order for my soul to exist. This is a must for all living beings, for anything else is stagnation, disease eventually leading to death.

By standing on the edge of my comfort zone, I learnt I had a choice. One, to move forward and step out into the field of possibilities and accept my current reality, or two, remain in what I know and go home to the familiar and certainty.

In the past, when I was confronted by this moment of choice between head and heart, I would feel paralysed in the middle of a crossroads. Neither path seemed appealing, both with their equal amount of negatives and positives. When I made a list on any situation, my mind could be quite powerful in creating whatever pros and cons I needed to see in order to not move forward into uncertainty.

Ultimately, for my ego to be satisfied, the choice was the easiest and safest. It was very clever that way, protecting me from any kind of shaky ground. Ego trickery I call this. The ego is clever it can manipulate you into seeing uncertainty as unsafe. Once again, I realised that courage was only found in facing the uncertainty and my fears. That is what following our dharma or heart is asking us to do: overcome, shift, grow, expand, become.

It was in this space I learnt about faith.

Faith brings in a feeling of calmness in the face of chaos. Sometimes we cannot know what is over the mountain until we have walked over it. This does not make the journey any more pleasant. It can still be harrowing, even life threatening, however still necessary to grow and get to our destination. In ancient times, even survival depended on it. Eventually we will get a view from the top and breathe a sigh of relief as our gaze and the possibilities are widened once more.

In just about every journey and story since the beginning of time – from the greatest explorers, prophets and leaders of our world – there were moments where all seemed lost. When they question whether or not to turn back, challenged to their very core. In all these stories, the gold was received only when they faced that fear of nothingness and uncertainty and went forward with faith and courage into the unknown.

I am reminded at this moment of a beautiful movie I saw in Nepal called 'Caravan', a story about a boy living high in Mustang region of Nepal who had never seen a tree. He was determined to see one. Every year, his father set off on another harrowing, dangerous journey down through the Himalayas; herding yaks through treacherous mountain passes and wild weather. He'd always ask, 'Father, please can I come with you? I would love to see a tree.'

Each year, his father declined in order to keep him safe, until one year he snuck along behind them. The story shows all the trials of the journey, and even the boy's father dies, however in the end the boy sees the tree. It was worth it in the end, forever changed by the harrowing journey and the loss along the way.

Our soul's desires do not go away. They will wait for eternity if they have to, patiently, gently asking, repeatedly, over and over until we take action. Our job is to listen and hear the call of our heart and trust it, to have faith that we will be guided, just as this boy was. He suffered along the way, but it was his time to see the tree. A truth seeker will always see the truth of all things, the shadow and light, the suffering and joy and, in that, will find wisdom and lead others to freedom as well.

Unfortunately, so many of us turn back at the point when we are just about to be on the up. I remember sitting so long in the belly of the deepest black hole in despair and overwhelm, moving from anxiety to depression, and back again. The moment I started to move and accept where I was, things always started flowing again and new challenges were thrown at me.

Then, as the biggest hurdle came, once again I'd turn back and hang on to the old, safe and known territory. I'd go back into the darkness of unknowingness and powerlessness, getting worn out from recycling the same old energy and not getting anywhere, recreating and reliving old patterns.

The change and shift came when I started to have faith, faith that I was part of the 'whole', something bigger than me. Whenever we follow our hearts, our hearts may lead us into uncharted territory or rough waters; this is part of the preparation for opening ourselves up to the new changes ahead.

Nature teaches us beautifully that everything is a cycle. All we have to do is flow with it and go with it. It is important to accept the winter and work with that as much as the spring and summer. So, as Susan Jeffers writes in her book, 'Fear and challenge always come before change and success', it is okay to 'feel the fear and do it anyway'.

When we follow our hearts, we are allowing our soul's path to guide us through life. All feelings of regret, frustration and hopelessness leave us because we see possibilities where darkness had been. When we truly follow our hearts, I believe we are following our dharma, the DNA, the genetics, all the things, the tools, that perfectly align to create you at this point in time. To fill you with energy, a purpose, a responsibility to show up and play the role assigned to you for this life's journey.

In fact, we are in a relationship with everything and everyone on this planet. There are invisible threads that bind us all. It reminds me of a game where you have a ball of thread and you ask people in the room a question; if they agree that they have had that experience, they get the end of the string and you connect all the people who share that experience with the same thread. You then repeat the process over and over and before long, everyone in the room is connected to everybody. This is a great exercise for us all to understand our planet. WE are ALL connected! If it affects the planet, it will affect you and vice versa.

Acceptance, compassion, and forgiveness are only natural when we recognise this relationship with all things. It becomes part of who we are when we start to follow this path and this energy expands, so we have more purpose and love in our lives.

It is easier to accept the suffering or pain in our own lives when we surrender to our hearts, because everything comes from a place of love. We cannot judge when we live in the loving place of the heart. We are kinder to ourselves. We are gentler and allow mistakes. Therefore, we can move on, being compassionate, growing and changing faster, becoming more of who we are. Becoming more whole, more humble, ultimately showing up in the world with more grace and humility, because we understand that it all has purpose.

This does not mean we can condone bad behaviour. What it does is help us choose a more loving pathway for ourselves and those around us.

To follow our hearts is inviting us to be courageous, to be vulnerable, to have 'faith'. To let go of the conditions and expectations of how things 'should' be and accept how things 'are'. To work with what is and realise that we can only control or change the way 'we' behave or take action at any given moment.

We do not have to be the victims of patterns, systems, and ways of being that do not support our highest calling, best self or dharma. To fall in love with the journey, where you are and the process, not the destination. To recognise the powerful difference between expectations and choosing to appreciate. True freedom and love exist in the place of appreciation, gratitude, and love.

Personally, this is still an area I am exploring and learning, to not fear the uncertainty. No matter how treacherous the journey or choices may seem from my current viewpoint, I have faith that it will lead me to where I need to go, and so far, it has.

Following my dharma has led me to love. In that space of expansive uncertainty and beauty, I dropped all expectations and just appreciated the soul before me. I found the courage in the darkest parts of my soul and thankfully, was able to recognise what it was asking me to do.

Every time fear arose – the fear of rejection, of judgment, or the feeling of I do not deserve – I saw it as an opportunity to love more, give more, appreciate more, and become more vulnerable. With this action, love came back to me and I could recognise it, and go deeper than ever before.

If we can truly grasp the understanding that love and fear are two sides of the same coin, we can start to experience everything as an expression of love. All of it is part of us. Our shadow self needs to be loved and brought into the light, not rejected or oppressed, as this will surely result in the expression of that fear in ways that can only cause destruction. Get vulnerable. It is the surest way to expand and experience love.

> *'Expansion and contraction, Love and Fear are just two sides of the same coin. When we integrate the ultimate truth of this relationship, we can truly connect and move into oneness. We are then in relationship with the cosmos.'*
>
> KATE HANSSEN BOHARA

Chapter 5
Expansion and Contraction

Really imagine the birth process, from conception to birth. It starts with a thought, a seed, an intention, sometimes an act of love, or in some cases force. The foetus forms with fertilisation and then the growth starts. Each stage of development is important, and the foetus cannot progress to the next stage without completing the first.

As it grows through the stages, the mother is also changing, adapting, growing, and preparing for her new chapter. In a sense she is also developing through the stages, preparing for the birth and the new role of mother. The foetus slowly takes form and as both it and the mother-to-be grow, people respond to them in a new way, negative or positive, depending on the circumstances around the event.

It can be exciting to witness creation and equally scary. For example, the earthquake in Nepal was an expression of mother earth's expansion and contraction. Scary from our perspective, however, the very beauty of the Himalayas has been forged through these natural events over millions of years. No matter how creation has occurred, it still deserves and invites appreciation and love.

In this moment, there is pure potential and possibility. After nine months of expansion, the mother-to-be and child start experiencing a lot of discomfort. The child has got no more room to expand, and the mother-to-be is experiencing this tightening as well. How much more can her body stretch and change? How much longer can she carry this weight?

Suddenly, the body responds, the contractions start, pain, more discomfort and both the baby and mother are uncomfortable and are being pushed to move or change. Interestingly, as the contractions are occurring, the mother's body is preparing to give birth. It knows what to do; it needs no instruction, and it is expanding at the same time as contracting.

After the contractions become almost too intense to bear and the mother questions her ability to physically birth this baby, she finally pushes the baby out into the world with a multitude of feelings moving through her. There can be feelings of overwhelm, hopelessness, anger, and unbearable pain. Feelings of relief, elation and joy follow as the baby takes its first breath.

A new chapter begins, full of potential and possibility. Is this not our first experience of being a human and our preparation for this journey on earth? Our birthing experience perfectly encapsulates and prepares us for the very life we will have on a daily, monthly or annual cycle and throughout many milestones in our lives. At the end of each cycle, we experience discomfort, pain, irritation or frustration, only to experience relief, joy and elation as we get through the other side and start creating and expanding again.

After every negative experience, is a positive one. Govin often reminds me as I experience my own birth, life and death cycles. 'Baby, the sun will always rise in the east and set in the west, and every month the moon will appear full again.'

It is my fear that keeps me trapped in suffering and resistance. When I resisted, I was going against nature. I was literally still existing in my mother's uterus, not wanting to leave the comfort of the known world of foetal reality. Despite being pushed and contracted upon, I was holding on for dear life, refusing to let go of the known, to avoid the unknown. Quite a grotesque thought, when we put it like this, but I think you get my point.

So too, if the mother resists the pain of childbirth, it is a documented fact that she will most likely need intervention and medical help in birthing. We are existing in both the macro and micro. Birth, life, and death cycles continuously move and change throughout our lives and always will. We will always move through cycles of development, learning and growing, the cycles that always end in contraction and a rebirth of sorts, destruction and creation, before we can be reborn and expand once again with a new set of experiences to propel us forward on our journey.

Through observation, my journey, and working with people from all walks of life as a counsellor, trainer and mentor, one thing has stood out for me: a common denominator about depression.

It has led me to ask a series of questions within myself and also of the external world. I feel that creativity and depression are linked. I feel that our modern society is mirroring back to us the gap that exists within each individual, the disconnectedness from the soul or authentic self or god self. The part of us that is nature, the part of us that is instinctual or creation.

If we are not connected with this part of ourselves, then how can we be connected to anything? Possibly resulting in depression/ disconnection from life, ourselves, those we love. The more perceived struggles a person has, the less space they have to create, as the walls feel like they are closing in. The vision narrows, which further limits possibility and opportunity. In other words, there is a perception of having no choice. This is a result of belief systems that have passed their use-by date and, more often than not, are a result of stubbornness or fear of change.

The ego is hanging on so tight to outdated ideals, creating further discomfort, disease, disconnection, and limitation. Actually, if we can learn to sit in this feeling, becoming conscious of how to be in harmony with it, non-judging, appreciating and observing it as a wave of change, then we can often ride that wave and the challenge is not as hard as previously thought.

When I learnt to integrate or download new knowledge and experiences, I could then rearrange and reframe old beliefs or perceptions. This enabled me to create and move forward, expanding once more, moving.

People sometimes get so stuck in the bottom of the well looking into the black abyss below that they forget to look up and see the light. While ever we can see the light, there is hope, there is something possible, potentially outside of us we can welcome in.

The word 'depression' or 'depressed' is commonly heard in conversations today and is used to describe just about any emotion or feeling that is the opposite of happy. It seems to me people enjoy having this word to describe how they are feeling without actually tuning into the feeling.

I felt I had forgotten the language of my feelings of my soul and because I had slipped into so much automation and speed of life, I no longer took the time to feel emotions fully and express myself clearly. This made me think back to a time when letters were written as a form of communication and people had to wait months on end to receive one love letter. How much expression of feeling do you think they had in them? I can only imagine that people wrote everything they felt, as this may have been the last or only opportunity for them to express themselves. At that time, I have no doubt the threads that connected us to each other were solid, and you held deep connections with loved ones.

In the past, artists were seen as gifted and important for the same reason. They were celebrated for their ability to see and feel so deeply, and then be able to express those feelings on canvas, or in music or dance. They brought beauty, appreciation, joy and the energy of possibility and creation. They made way for the daydreams. The imagination had somewhere to play.

During my first marriage, I had lost the connection to those parts of myself and noticed like many people, I wanted to label and box things up into neat little packages and give them names to identify and file away. Creating the illusion, I was somehow in control and knew all there was to know about that little box.

 linked this way of being to the mindset of quick fixes. I'm too busy for that and all the sicknesses of modern society that are about the magic happy pill. We all want the magic happy pill. We should always be happy, right? Nowadays, I think many people are so scared of feeling negative emotions; they think any emotion that lingers too long is depression, then pass that label around as easily as drinking water. We are so scared of our shadow selves that we continuously oppress ourselves and each other, preventing any real connection or real communication. Catapulting ourselves further into that feeling of loneliness or modern depression.

Don't you think it is strange that people go to the doctor because they are sad all the time? Ever done this and noticed when they diagnose depression or anxiety and prescribe the medication to help, there is suddenly a mild relief about having a label for the feelings and a pill to fix it? This is our ego's happiness. Now it has a legit excuse to maintain control and a reason for feeling that way and feeling powerless.

In that space, we can now be a victim and have a reason for feeling lonely and sad. Think for a moment, how does this scenario empower anyone to make a change or take responsibility for what they 'can' do rather than what they 'can't' do? It doesn't.

It keeps them locked in a cycle of powerlessness.

Now I am not saying we can't be depressed, I'm suggesting that there are better alternatives to working 'with' this energy than suppressing it. I'm suggesting that modern depression is a symptom of disconnection from self, the lack of true relationship with self, the environment, with others, and spirit.

Depression becomes this blanket term that describes any feeling that brings us down. I am not saying to not use medicines. They have their place, of course, temporarily, in clinical and deepseated, long-term issues. However, I definitely advocate that we need to change our perceptions and attitudes about this over diagnosed condition, which, in my view, is part of being human, a symptomatic expression that something needs to change.

I believe we need to take responsibility for how we are allowing our egos to run rampant, conjuring all sorts of limitations; creating what I like to call modern world depression. Let's look at the cause before addressing the symptoms. I honestly believe the epidemic of mental health issues in this modern society is in direct proportion to the dysfunction in it and our disconnection to who and what we really are: spiritual beings having a human 'being' experience.

With this in mind, I'd like to propose the following. Depression is a dip in the road. An opportunity to take a rest, a time for reflection, a place to go within, away from the chaos in the world. A time for a holiday, to go walkabout, to meditate, a curveball, to contemplate, or space to create. Perhaps it is to retreat, to stop the fighting and the struggle. Allow yourself to feel, to deconstruct without judgment, with open, loving arms, like you would embrace an emotional child.

When we deconstruct, we allow ourselves space to feel. Imagine tipping a bucket of stagnant water out (water being the suppressed emotions) and then the bucket is lighter to carry. If you really feel like you are in depression, this is your soul's way of telling you some major changes need to happen. You are resisting the contractions and expansion. You are not working with the birthing process; you are resisting your very nature. Your core beliefs need a shake up and you need to have a new experience. Your perceptions need to shift. A new view is required.

I say new experience, because to be honest, as I shared earlier about my self-help phase, as much as that helped me in some ways, it was that combined with a physical experience that had the biggest impact on my life.

My most profound lessons, changes and biggest shifts occurred when I got courageous enough to physically step into the unknown. Becoming the explorer of my own inner world led me to becoming an explorer of my outer world. I gained a new appreciation for my world. The most life altering experience being Nepal. Nepal changed me forever in ways I that are still unfolding today.

In other cultures around the world, such as Asia, depression is not recognised in quite the same way. It is looked upon as being a more physical issue. Stephen Lau from 'Depression and the Oriental Health' writes: 'from a Chinese medicine perspective, depression is largely related to the stagnation of liver "qi" (Qi is internal life energy coursing through the physical body, nourishing your body cells with life-giving oxygen. When there is blockage, instead of smooth flowing 'qi', disease and disorder occur)'.

In Ayurveda, they would call this Prana. As such Ayurveda talks about our relationship with everything – our food, our environment, people, our perspectives, and more. It understands that depression and disease are most likely a lack of life force, prana flowing in an area of the body, and this is affected by all the above.

An example of this is your liver. It is not only the fat processor of the body, but it is also related to the emotions of anger and frustration. Emotions can affect the way your liver functions and vice versa. It is important we learn how to manage our anger and frustration. Stress management plays a critical role. What we do for stress management may differ from person to person, as we all have different constitutions and different elements that make us up.

Interestingly to note, in conjunction with ancient texts, scientists are considering the link between nutrition and mental health. Scientists are confirming what the Ayurvedic doctors and Chinese doctors have been saying for thousands of years; we literally are what we eat.

Modern lifestyles of fast food and fast lives have created mineral deficiencies. The lack of freshly prepared food with local produce, what I call 'life force food', is contributing to mental health issues along with physical health issues. It makes sense that live food is more beneficial for our gut health than anything processed.

Gut health is fast becoming the link to a lot of modern diseases and mental health conditions. It can be traced to pesticides, chemicals and other processes that interfere with food composition, therefore it would interfere with our system as well.

Whilst living in Nepal, I became aware of the way they communicated with each other, which I will share more of later in this book. One of the most common phrases I heard when people spoke was 'Tapai eklai chha?', which means are you alone? In Nepal, everything centres around belonging and community. They are very aware of the vulnerability that exists when you are alone. So they are always with people, supporting and connecting with each other in the community. To them, society is everything. If people are alone in Nepal, they know something is very wrong and that this person is having a really bad time and needs help.

I noticed whilst living in Nepal, especially after the earthquake, that the whole community reflected this sense of 'we are all in this together'. I think this experience has played a major role in reshaping how I view not only my own path in life but also of the wider community.

Together we 'belong', we matter and are valued. We have a role to play, once again affirming this notion of 'relationship', Brene Brown, the scientist who has found her way into studying human behaviour and connection, has recently been talking about the importance of belonging. That true connection comes from a sense of belonging. Belonging to a tribe, a clan, a family, a club, or society.

Within this space of belonging, humans can find their role, and they can matter. They have a value, and that makes a significant difference in our state of being and how we relate to our world. The only problem is that in our modern societies, this sense of belonging has been lost with the rise of capitalism, individualism, and the need to succeed.

These days I often seek to be alone and enjoy the solitude, however this is a choice thing. I choose this, almost like meditation, a retreat, or to 'connect' with me. I would say this is the result of living in a country like Australia where there is so much stimulation and busy-ness all the time; that to balance it out, sometimes I seek solitude. Aloneness in this way can be empowering, creative, and healing. However, it is very different to 'loneliness', which is born out of disconnection, cutting off our values and living in disharmony with ourselves and our lives.

A little tip on how to improve your connection.

I noticed that when I started to feel overwhelmed, due to modern life taking over my thoughts and emotions, that I had this internal alarm clock, alerting me to take time out, to take a step back from the madness of the world. It would show up as what most people would perceive as a negative emotion. If this negative emotion came up and stayed around, I would notice it like an alarm clock and realise it was telling me to I needed to pay attention.

I would ask myself, 'is this behaviour, activity or thought form serving me right now?'

'Is it helping me to be the best version of myself?'

'Does this behaviour, activity or thought have love in it?'

Those three questions would always bring me closer to my centre. They would assist me to step off the treadmill of automatic thinking for a moment. I would become the observer of myself.

In feeling these feelings and asking myself these questions, I moved from a place of limitation and suppression to a place of expansion. I listened to myself. I heard and validated my feelings. I became my own counsellor. The next step was to breathe and usually, I would take a break in nature, and this would be enough to reset and reconnect.

A few years ago, just before heading to Nepal, I was feeling overwhelmed by increasing pressure to have a job, maintain a mortgage, be a single mum to four children, and somehow keep my creativity alive.

I could feel myself getting more weighed down and losing my enthusiasm for life again. My soul was dying a slow death. I was finding it hard to get out of bed and lacked energy for everything. I could not handle any complex issues. My thoughts became self-defeating, and I was feeling trapped and oppressed by my situation, stuck.

I was not only self-sabotaging, but my lack of energy and purpose was also affecting my children and the people I cared most about. This created guilt within me and further fuelled what would, no doubt, be diagnosed as depression.

I stopped cooking, cleaning, and being social. I withdrew further into myself in a negative way, becoming numb. I had been trying to straddle the fence for too long. I was constantly juggling the 'shoulds' and my 'soul's desires', creating suffering, disillusionment, and disconnection.

I woke up extremely frustrated one day, tired, head aching and with feelings of giving up. I went for a walk on the beach and had a million negative and conflicting thoughts in my head.

After a while, I stopped, took a breath, and sat down. I looked out across the expansive and wild ocean. The view always soothed me somewhat and today was no different. Immediately I felt small. That feeling of insignificance was enough to get me to breathe and relax a little, shedding a tear at the beauty of it, the recognition that whatever I was struggling with was nothing in the infinite universe and it would pass like the waves. The mountains and expansive views and space in the Himalayas did the same thing. It was always like the ocean had something to say; it had something to remind me. It was showing me that there was this huge space, full of potential and possibility. Suddenly the walls that had been closing in started to crumble and I let the ocean in.

The ocean filled me with its potential, with its power and its hugeness. I was being limited by my own thoughts and actions. I was crying, but they were tears of joy and sadness, both in recognition of my soul, the sadness of ignoring it for so long. Quietly I spoke to my heart, 'tell me what I need to do? I am listening'. You see, I had not listened in a long time. The very intention of listening at this moment was enough for the channel to open. I waited, just breathing, closing my eyes, emptying my mind of all thoughts, and listened to the ocean in front of me.

After about five minutes of silence, I heard it very quietly, but I heard it. The answer came, and I knew instantly it was for me because it came from this space of expansion with the ocean. It didn't come from desperation or fear, it came from surrendering. It felt expansive, it felt infinite, it felt full of possibility and, most of all, the energy I had been missing returned suddenly. I think they call this inspiration (spirit in action).

Every time I spoke about or thought about the answers I had received that day, I could feel the surge of excitement at the possibilities and infinite potential that surrounded me. No longer did I feel trapped and powerless. I felt empowered and excited about what was coming. Despite the uncertainty of it all, the details were irrelevant.I did not need those, as I knew they'd be delivered at the right moment.

The details are not important. As most people will tell you, depression is not caused by one thing. People are not often depressed because of one event. It is usually the slow breaking down of old paradigms of thinking that no longer serve us.

I believe depression is here to show us ourselves and what we are capable of. It is the compass of our dharma. It asks us to look at how we are being and change our view, look out a different window. It is asking us to flip it! It's asking us to look deeper without fear of who we are and embrace it. To have faith, courage and surrender to the guidance that is with us always. It is asking us to listen.

The length of time we stay in depression is based on our resistance to feeling it or acknowledging that something needs to change. I have been learning through my life's journey to work with depression and use it for my creative pursuits. It doesn't mean I am never sad, or glum, or challenged, or feel grief.

The key, I have found, is to feel and to understand the feelings, get to know your feelings and do not fear them. They are there to help you stay true to your heart and be a human being, full of infinite potential and expansiveness. Limitation and suppression are created by fear of ourselves, of our potential. It is all a matter of perception. Depression is a necessary tool for our understanding of 'SELF' and to keep us connected with our journey. It has a purpose if we let it. It is the shadow that needs to be brought to the light.

Chapter 6
I Do Believe In Fairy Tales, I Do, I Do….

Once upon a time I believed in 'happily ever after'. I believed when I went to family gatherings and saw all the smiles and hugs, that those families were happy and this was how all healthy families should look, one hundred per cent of the time. My family was good at that, putting on masks. Much later, as I grew up, I learned that families always had dark secrets, pain and suffering hidden behind those masks. But until I acknowledged my own mask, I could not see theirs. I loved watching the Shrek movie with my kids, a culmination of all those fairy tales rolled into one. Like so many of us growing up, these fairy tale ideals have been met with a lot of disappointment and disillusionment in our modern societies. I believe we have lost the art of relating and understanding what partnerships, relationships look like or more importantly feel like.

I guess some might say I was naïve and oblivious to the truths that went on behind all the chocolate birthday cakes and parties. Families are all dysfunctional in love, there is no 'normal'. We love each other from all sorts of spaces. From wanting control and certainty, possession, fear, and many other places that many of us are not even aware of. Our sub-conscious needs and desires are endlessly trying to manipulate our relationships all the time to suit our needs. Then when our needs or expectations are not met, we get angry, frustrated or feel like they don't love us in the way we want them to. You see, we all seem to have conditions on what love should look like; based on our upbringing and possibly the narratives in our romance movies and fairy tales have had a part to play too. It is part of the ego that we, as humans, are here to master. It is in our DNA to repeat family patterns of the unconscious. Unless we bring them to the light, to the conscious mind, we will continue to be slaves to the shadows of the past. By being unconscious, we are destined to repeat family patterns, thought forms, and maintain the same level of understanding about life and love.

Looking back on my childhood, I often felt like an alien. I remember looking to the skies and talking to whomever and whatever might be out there, listening and asking questions about this thing we earthlings call 'life'. I remember talking to 'god' whatever that may be and I often felt closer to my idea of 'god' than I did to other human beings or their notions of what 'god' was.

I never liked religion. I remember coming home from school at age eight and declaring to my mother that I did not want to do R.E. (religious education) because I felt the stories were not real. I remember feeling like the lady reading these biblical stories was lying and manipulating us. She seemed hypocritical to me and judgmental and I guess that was enough for me to decide religion was not for me. I did art class instead. So even though I was always in communion with God in some way (my way) I definitely was never going to follow blindly a religious faith and trust other people's ideas of what 'god' was. Looking back at this, I feel that this was in my DNA, possibly from my grandfather's side.

I recall a story he told me about religion and faith and how he changed his views on it all after the Second World War. He told me that for many years, he was a devout Catholic follower and that he had three significant experiences that made him question his faith. The last and most significant being that his local priest announced in front of the Sunday congregation that the child he recently lost prior to baptism would not ascend to heaven as it was not baptised. I imagine the imprint of that experience is definitely recorded in my DNA somewhere.

In my childhood, I remember observing many adults and families go about their robotic lives. They never seemed to question their actions and seemed very purposeful. I recall asking these adults about their routine activities often: 'Why do we have to go to school?', 'Can't you teach me?', 'Why do we have to have money?', 'Or work nine to five?'.

In my mind, I was often thinking, surely there is a better way to do this? I did not understand so much of what modern life was about. It always seemed so strange and disconnected. I always felt like we were missing out on so much.

Most adults looked at me disapprovingly, and told me I was 'living in the clouds' and to get back to reality, or they'd say, 'well what else should we be doing?' In which case I often had loads of answers, yet they laughed and scoffed at me like I was a naïve child, and even though I was in many ways, some part of me felt my questions were valid. They would often say 'you're off with the fairies'. I think at that moment, I decided whenever I could be 'off with the fairies' then I would be and play in my imagination. At least that would bring me some possibility and inspiration. To be connected to the tribe, I had to keep expression and thoughts to myself! I made a point of balancing daydreaming, observing, and conforming to fit into the tribe. I learnt to live mirroring my family, local society and the uninspiring Australian TV.

I loved reading stories, especially ones like Enid Blyton's 'The Magic Faraway Tree' and 'The Wishing Chair Adventures'. I felt as if I was in them. I was flying, visiting faraway places, meeting exotic people, and having a wondrous time. These stories would fuel my imagination and help me to believe that there was something wondrous to connect to beneath the humdrum life of school, sport and modern Australia country life.

I was lucky enough to own horses and would chat to my pony daily. I believed we were communicating. We would go on long rides in the Yarra Valley countryside near my home, and this was always an adventure. My imagination would once again dance to the possibilities. Horse riding was such free time for me, allowing me to explore and pretend I was an explorer, finding new and exciting places that others had not found yet.

That part of my childhood was full of adventure, freedom, and exploration. I resisted being 'brought down to earth' at school and I resisted my parents' attempts to reality check me from time to time. By the time my sister and I were fourteen, we were still playing with Legos and Barbie dolls. I guess I liked and enjoyed living in my fluffy cloud world. In this place, I was an explorer, wandering the lands and learning about different far-off places, people, and their ways. I knew most of the major countries of the world, their capital cities and their flags. When anyone asked me what I wanted to do in life as in a career, I always answered in one word 'travel'.

I could tell you many stories of our imagination-fuelled play times; from haunted shacks in the bush, to fairies that lived in mushrooms and horse-riding adventures that took us days to complete. In short, despite the adapting environment and the world needing us to grow up, we resisted, and my creative side was not too damaged, despite it being suppressed deep inside by school and the busyness of modernity.

Observing the adults, my peers, and society, I often had questions. I remember asking my mother about the ozone layer and child poverty. I even wrote a letter to Prime Minister Bob Hawke about pollution when I was nine. My mother always told me not to worry about those things, to just be nine and go play. I guess I had a global consciousness even then and now it is clear to me, that even then, my dharma was trying to reveal itself.

I remember telling myself that Australia was safe and that living here was safe from natural disasters.

I told myself not to think of the animals that were suffering as you cannot do anything about this, so don't think about it. (I guess this was an example of my small life in a small town, believing there was not much outside of this to aim for, as in I was powerless to do anything, I was small.)

I could not even watch Bambi as a child without crying, let alone Lassie, Skippy, and Phar Lap. Subsequently, these days I am predominantly vegetarian and still learning about better ways to be in the world and practice Ahimsa (harm nothing).

I think it was a learnt behaviour; that if I did not like the feeling of something, then I would pretend it wasn't happening and go into my imagination and distract myself. It was easier than feeling small and powerless. One of the ways to distract myself from the world and filter out the negativity, was to be social and invite others into my space all the time. I became a socialite and a brilliant chameleon, fitting in to anything just to distract myself, just like my family and everyone else I learnt to put on that mask. Failing that, there was TV.

Having children young and running off to Western Australia for real-life adventures meant I was able to continue connecting to the childhood wonders through my children. I believe that despite the sudden jerk into motherhood responsibilities, my children benefited from my youthful outlook and imagination. Santa and I really did have board meetings on a regular basis to discuss the logistics of next Christmas and who would receive presents.

My twenties and early thirties were spent battling the inner conflict of my inner child's needs and my adult needs. It seemed the gap between the two was growing. There was a separation of self and this so-called depression the doctor diagnosed me with, which, after my third child was gradually becoming more dominating. I needed help.

This, of course, played out in many scenarios. Particularly and most prominently in my relationship, as my teenage inner child was rebelling against my adult self and, in turn, my first husband. I could not conform to the perceived 'normality' that was being played out all around me. There was always this feeling that I was here to do more, experience more, feel more, and be more.

At around twenty-nine, I was angry, frustrated, confused, and disgusted with the outside world. The worst part was, I no longer had an escape to my imagination or other creative pursuits. I felt like all my walls had been infiltrated. There was nowhere to retreat to anymore. I'd forgotten to see the fairies and life had made me feel without purpose. I was a full-time mother of three and was struggling to even know my own needs in favour of their's and their father's. I was trying so hard to please everyone and, most of all, displeasing myself. I was disconnected, physically, mentally, emotionally and definitely spiritually.

Looking back, this was the time I lost faith in the fairy tale. However, my child self still believed in it and would fight hard for the diminishing spark of it that was laying in the recesses of my subconscious. There was a distinct inner battle of dragons and princesses between structure and freedom.

I started exploring the idea of 'connection'. At first, it was through nature, meditation, music, and art. I joined classes that taught psychic development, reiki, healing, and all manner of things that started to reignite me. Slowly, slowly, I started to reconnect with parts of me I had lost and suppressed. My emotions started flowing again, and I began to feel and reconnect with things around me. I saw 'god' or 'spirit' or whatever you want to call it in the little things – birds singing, butterflies, flowers. I revisited nature in a new way with child-like wonderment and I started to reconnect, I was beginning a relationship with me again.

I was feeling more naked than ever before, more vulnerable and certainly less together, however it was different. I felt more at peace about it, playful even, an acceptance of humanness and its flaws. I'd stopped being so hard on myself. The feeling that it was okay to be imperfect or an unfinished piece of art. It is funny how art imitates life, and this is evident to me now more than ever. I used to get quite impatient and panicked at the thought of showing my unfinished art, my writing, my unclean house. I was embarrassed about my imperfections. It was like I became more okay with the process of becoming the more I leant in to appreciating the beauty that is in everything. The more I loved out there, the more I loved and accepted inside me. I allowed myself to be in the process and also be of the process. This was a new place for me.

Fast forward to the last few years and I feel I have finally climbed down out of the tower that I had built myself into. I am no longer waiting like Rapunzel for her saviour. I said goodbye to the idea of a Prince Charming and wandered off into the forbidden forests myself, seeking new adventures.

Finding my own white horse and being fearless to ride alone with no approval or acceptance.

It felt like a new chapter. Which got me thinking, I am going to live my life as if I was writing a book. I am creating the characters, the scene, the location, the tone, the everything. This made me feel more powerful and slowly I started unshackling myself. My role was changing. I felt guided, like I was being urged to create something lasting. Something I could leave behind for others to stumble upon and perhaps even assist them on their journey. I was here to inspire my children, to show them through actions, not words.

I tended to be impatient. As contradictory as it sounds, I was also a procrastinator, who busied myself with menial tasks to distract myself from what I really want to do. Subconsciously, it was because I was stuck on the 'how', I was always worried about doing it wrong. I most certainly did not want to pass that on to my kids.

The truth is, do we ever know how? I don't think we ever really know how. We learn on the job and here I am once again, learning on the job.

Chapter 7
Nurturing the Seeds

Everything that exists was a seed of the imagination. The imagination sets us apart from other creatures on this planet; it allows us to manifest and create from our dreams, visions and inspiration.

We form our core beliefs in the first seven to nine years of our existence on this planet. Multiple religions all agree in part about this point, and many psychologists too, as far as we develop and integrate knowledge through our experiences both through nature and nurture. We are developing our perceptions and views based on the experience we have. Is the planet a safe place or is there something to fear?

Scientists have studied the way people develop through the study of twins. They observed how they developed over time in different families, and different environments and the impact that had on the development of their DNA, behaviour, choices, beliefs and so on. We now know to be true a belief that is held on to for a long time without being challenged can become a concrete belief. Therefore, it is often harder to break habits or learn new things the older we get. With the developmental stages of children, that first seven to nine years can be crucial in how they develop as adults and whether they go into life; believing they can or believing they can't.

People can get stuck in holding patterns that become so stagnant that they stop growing and become the victims of a concrete reality. If you look hard enough at people's bodies and how they develop, you can see the manifesting of their thoughts in the way their bodies are taking shape. This can be seen in their bodies and minds as illness, structure, and ability. A very stuck and stagnant life will eventually lead to a very stagnant and stuck body. Eventually, patterns of behaviour can become so automatic and integrated that they become rigid, concrete.

To encourage healthy growth in people, we need to be aware of the patterns repeating themselves as habits, family patterns, genetics, and disease. We need to become conscious of our core beliefs; transforming and transcending them when we are being challenged to do so by listening to our thoughts, actions, and behaviours. When we are triggered or challenged, this is a clue that our belief systems are being challenged or being asked to shift and evolve. Everything has something to teach us. We are gathering tools for our tool box continuously. However, what good are the tools if we don't figure out how to use them or worse still, not even recognise that we have accumulated them?

Like planting fresh seeds (fresh ideas and thoughts), once they are sown, we have to nurture them; we have to give energy to them every day. We tend to our creation and understand that it is at its most vulnerable in the early stages and thus grows stronger and more real, the more effort and energy we put into it. Just like our thoughts. The difference is, when we think a negative thought, we are undoing or affecting the growth of that particular seed.

Here is a little tip on how to connect with your Inner Garden.

An inner Garden meditation

You have to imagine that the thoughts you choose to anchor into reality are the things that will grow and manifest into your life in some form. Like a spiral or vortex that speeds up and gathers momentum.

Closing your eyes with a piece of paper in front of you and some coloured pencils. Taking deep breaths, get into a state of relaxation.

Imagine your inner world is like a garden.

Take a few moments of scanning the garden and getting a feel for the type of garden. Is it an organised garden? A vegie garden? A rose garden? A Japanese garden? A wild forest? Paying attention to all the little details, such as, if there is water there, what type of water body? Is it clean? Dirty? Running? Still?

Now look into that garden. How are you tending to it? This will help you to see how you tend to yourself. What state is it in?

Is it cared for? Where would you like to focus on it? Perhaps you're making a new garden bed? What sort?

What will you grow? What is growing? Is it what you want in there?

You could meditate on this for a few minutes if you like, asking all manner of questions about your garden. Then, using a large sheet of paper, draw, write or sketch, about your garden noting as many details as possible and then really look at it and notice all the parts of it.

What's in the shadows? Are the trees big or small? Is it a lush garden or a sparse dying garden filled with weeds?

All the answers you receive regarding your garden give you an opportunity to see what's being created in your mind. Where you may be tending too much in one area and not in another. Perhaps your garden is not being tended to at all. This will help you see whether your seed nurturing, or intention setting, is taking place. A gentle way to become aware of patterns of self-sabotage or neglect.

Understand, though, the importance of not allowing your mind to take control and think it knows better than the creation itself. The mind's job is always servant to the heart in creation. Its job is to provide structure, research, and support. It is not the decision maker or ruler. If you allow it to do that, you will often sabotage or destroy the very new seedling, a bit like a smothering mother or the other extreme, neglect it out of fear.

Chapter 8
Yin and Yang

Reading this proverb resonates with me on so many fronts. I was listening to Sadhguru. He was talking about the problem with forgetting our femininity – a big issue at the moment in western culture around women reclaiming their power. The fact is though, both men and women need the feminine and it exists in both of us in different ways. You see, feminine energy is the beauty in all things, the arts, the space where creation begins, the quiet, the being space. Masculine energy is the polar opposite, it is the action that completes the feminine inspiration. People today are missing what true femininity is. To me, this is a big part of what is out of balance in the world at the moment. Women and men have become equally masculine in their focus.

In the modern world, and possibly many other parts of the world, I feel the reason women are so angry and fighting for equality is we have lost faith in man's ability to protect us. I feel that over time man has got caught up in his power and come to abuse it and therefore, in varying degrees around the world, abused women too. Because to see their own vulnerability through the eyes of a woman is too much for them to bear, instead they'd rather oppress it. To see vulnerability in women is to see it in themselves. They fear it; they fear their own ability.

I understand women are feeling the need to be independent and their own protectors and providers, and want equality. For this reason, we have lost faith in the feminine aspect of ourselves and have turned to the masculine energy.

It is a two-pronged sword. By rising up to men, using the same energy they have used to oppress women, we are creating a bigger gap between men and women and therefore more war between the sexes. How we are fighting for equality is, in fact, destroying so much of what makes us women and, in turn, what makes them men. I feel women have become so fixated on gaining independence from men and men have become fixated on becoming successful at whatever the cost.

Both parties have lost their way, both are angry and frustrated, mirroring each other, mirroring the masculine energy in each of us. We have forgotten the connection to the divine mother; we have forgotten to see the beauty. We no longer understand the goddess and we no longer see value in the feminine values that once were revered in ancient societies. We need to remember who we really are. The answers are not to be found out there in the world in success and accolades, as so many of us seem to be obsessed with.

Please understand, I am not referring to the extreme cases and minority groups that have been abused or hurt by a 'male or female'. I am a big believer in healing things with love and connection. Therefore, I am suggesting we, as the majority, have a responsibility to love the hurt, educate, and empower. That is the only way.

I read about the way an African tribe issues punishment in their community. They bring the perpetrator into a circle surrounded by the whole community. Each community member expresses how the perpetrator's actions have hurt them personally and in what way. By the end of the session, the perpetrator is broken down with love, compassion, and forgiveness. The perpetrator becomes aware of himself and sees his own suffering through the suffering he witnessed and caused in the group. WOW. Powerful stuff. This really hit home for me. It is difficult for me to accept that punishments that increase pain and cause more suffering, more hatred and blame can heal, fix, change or support. It just

does not make sense to think that continuing the same action is going to get us a different result. Hatred and anger breed more of the same. Love and forgiveness allow expansion, growth, and healing.

Let's explore a bit more of this man versus woman subject.

Masculinity is physically strong, femininity is emotionally strong. Masculinity is scientific, logical and methodical, and femininity is intuitive, creative, artistic, empathic and compassionate. Masculinity is rigid and hard. Femininity is soft and supple. Equally, feminine and masculine energy coexists and interrelates in everything. A bit like Yin and Yang. A little bit of yin in every yang and vice versa. Masculinity needs femininity, it needs the Goddess, and femininity needs the masculinity of God.

It is so funny to me, talking to modern women as they complain about men not attending to their needs, or being the warrior they need, or ticking all the boxes. However, a man cannot be that when women keep taking masculine energy with this ever-present determination to be independent. Women are emasculating men everywhere. Then they wonder why men are becoming more withdrawn, selfish, and retreating to their man caves and not stepping up to be the man warrior hero that women desire.

We need to remember our relationship to the Divine not only universal divinity, but the divinity that flows through us as well. It is not separate; it is all part of the one, and if we do not recognise this soon, we will create a world of masculinity. Can you imagine a world with no beauty? Or no creativity? Just a continuous monotonous movement towards logic and reason. Some of you might be experiencing that in your worlds right now.

As we shift, transform, change, and move forward, perhaps it is time to revisit our roles on the planet and do what we are here to do. To stop judging and looking at ourselves as not enough, to see what we really are, what we can do, without the need to compete. We are here to complement each other, not compete with each other. Our journey is to find union, oneness, through the masculine and feminine. We have to make peace within ourselves and with each other by inviting the two energies into harmony. We need to reconnect to source and need to work with the earth.

Protect her and walk gently with her as she changes and shifts. It is not our role to restrict, force, or take from her. We can apply the Cherokee proverb to every aspect of life, even the planet. If we look at the feminine and masculine roles within us and then outside of us, we can see the expression of what we have neglected to nurture. If women do not feel protected like goddesses, then it is only natural they will want to become independent warriors themselves, further exasperating the problem.

If men are not revered and respected for their roles as protector and retriever, then they will look outside the relationship for another woman who needs protecting. This is instinctual, not learnt behaviour. Of course, if someone is born with varying degrees of masculine and feminine energy that is not necessarily aligned with their gender, then I would argue that perhaps they have a choice of which role they choose to play? Perhaps they feel more inclined towards one than another? The principle is the same, balance of the feminine and masculine within, and figuring out what is aligned and feels natural within.

Women are not protected or revered and are not free in many parts of the world. Unfortunately, the goddess energy has scared many of these cultures into suppressing women. It's more important to recognise they have suppressed the sacred feminine. They have misinterpreted the energy as a power and did not understand the true nature of it. In Nepal, I saw women being revered, valued and honoured for being mothers, grandmothers, sisters and daughters. It mattered less about the careers they chased or their expression of beauty. What mattered was their character and the care they gave to others close to them.

Despite the modern world's need to label countries such as this patriarchal, I have seen both sides. I believe the masculine power in these parts suppressed the feminine energy many thousands of years before. Feminine energy is powerful. It is both destruction and creation, and in part, it served the egos and men in power who let the power go to their heads to suppress this feminine power. Although if you spend time in some of these cultures, you will see hints of what I am talking about and the power that exists within these women is very feminine. Like the symbolism of the chalice and blade. Each has its purpose. Together they are complementary. Separated, they can be destructive; the blade slicing and cutting through and the chalice all-consuming and encompassing.

It is time to stop and reflect upon the myths, legends, proverbs, and ancient teachings in search of the wisdom that will assist us in rebalancing not only ourselves, but the planet too.

The goddess needs to return with the protection of the god within us all. Don't misunderstand me, I am referring to the masculine and feminine energy that exists in us all. Everything that is in our reality existed within us first.

You cannot be free to create and manifest unconditional love if you have to protect yourself all the time. It is counteractive energy. Love is to create, to trust, to open, and fear provokes the need for protection, to wield the sword. While we are busy spending millions of dollars on protection (fear), we cannot then spread love and compassion and create a harmonious planet.

'If you love a flower then, don't pick it up. Because if you pick it up it dies and ceases to be what you love.'

OSHO

Chapter 9
Fish Love

Self-love is only half of the picture. It is an energy like any other that is part of a whole. It has a shadow side. I mean, if you are loving self in equal measure, you need to love another. It is actually impossible to truly love self without loving your neighbours. The self-love that is often being talked about and expressed these days is not self-love, it is more self-obsession. It has been distorted to serve the mass marketing and consumerism that is ever present in our modern world. Energy is always ebbing and flowing, night and day, summer and winter, cycles are what we all are. So that once you have love, you have to give it away again, so that it may come back to you even bigger than before. It is constant giving and receiving.

Connect and contribute, disconnect and retreat. Then, through disconnection, connect again. Don't be afraid of disconnection. It is only in the spaces that we can create, integrate, reframe, and grow. This is why, when you love outside of yourself, after the honeymoon period, we start to feel this strange sadness. It reminds us that this current love exchange will transform at some point. It is a deep knowing that love is energy and therefore never stagnant. It will always be expanding, as that is what love does. To do this, we must be challenged. This is happening within and without. To hold on to love is suffocation, and the sure destruction of love. Love cannot be contained.

The current trend to focus on self-love is a bit misguided. It is good to recognise that deep within us all exists the love of life, and based on this, you will always naturally want to protect yourself and look after yourself. A lot of the love going around these days is what I would call selfish love. It is conditional love. It is not true love. I would argue that many people in modern society could or would not know 'true' love, even if they have it, because they do not recognise it. True love is expansive and at the same time can be contracting. It is all-encompassing, it is non-judgmental, it is responsive and unconditional. The fastest way to grow and expand is to give love away, not hold on to it.

Self-love is important, but not in the way it is being promoted. That is selfishness, and in all honesty, is creating the rise in narcissistic behaviour that is on the rise in the west. I feel we need to be aware of the role of self-love within relationship love, this is important. Without self-care, we get depleted and we cannot give, therefore struggling to give and receive love. There was a brilliant Black Mirror episode on Netflix called 'Nose-dive' which highlights this very well. We become so obsessed with receiving approval we mistake this for love. Spend thirty minutes on Instagram and you can see what I am talking about. All the advertising that exists at the moment prays on our desires and our need to get love, to get approval, to be accepted by the tribe. It is based on the feeling in us all of not being enough.

Most people express love through possession, ownership, and based on good behaviour. So typically, divorce rates have risen. Conditional marriages/conditional love. Maybe the question here is, if I give away all my love to the ones I love and get nothing in return, how do I feel? What would I do? If the answer has you feeling hurt, upset, or frustrated about not receiving in return, then you only understand selfish love. Self-love. I urge you to explore love, for love's sake. No expectations, no conditions, just allow yourself to feel the feeling of giving, and let that fill you up. Combine giving without expectation and loving yourself as you are, without the need to fill the voids with stuff and the approval of others. It is then you have the puzzle pieces in place to experience the full expansiveness of love. Love is always returned to us. In fact, it was never gone. It just transforms as we do and unfortunately, we are always looking for it with expectations, and focus where we think love is not. We put the conditions on what we think love should look like.

In a YouTube talk given by Sadhguru, he spoke about this simply. He said, 'So you catch the fish because you love to eat fish, but if you truly loved the fish, then why do you eat it?' This is a perfect example of modern-day love. Consumerism, possession is not love.

There's always a pot of gold at the end of the rainbow.

I had gotten used to spending time alone. I had slowly even found the courage to go out sometimes alone, even venturing to the Rainbow Serpent Festival one year, completely alone. Some part of me had decided that being alone was important for me at this time to get clear about who I was, but I think subconsciously, I was protecting myself. I was struggling, dealing with my own emotions and life, let alone anybody else's. I think I had worked out it was easier to hide when there was no mirror. I'd told myself I was self-Loving myself. Perhaps partly, I was caring for my fragile state. However, in equal measure, I was avoiding the shadow state, and therefore maintaining the illusion I was in control.

What an experience that festival was! The funniest experience I had alone, to be honest. After painting my face, I joined in with the meditation and yoga classes. I later danced with a new friend and then finally collapsed on the outside couches watching a trippy film on sexuality. I realised that I was more disconnected at that moment than ever. In my need to be independent and be okay with loneliness (myself), I'd become more comfortable being alone, which was great, but the very thing I needed was the opposite. I needed connection, intimacy and relationships, not just with myself but with others. I was actually taking the safe route. I had resurrected that relationship with myself, and it was time to connect with others again. I was playing it safe again; it was time for the next challenge.

The journey separating from my ex-husband had somewhat disconnected me from other people. All our friendship groups and community had virtually disappeared on the day we separated. In our case, the saying was true; you certainly find out who your real friends are. After the initial grief and sadness and months of trying to make sense of why people had reacted this way, I decided this realisation meant I could finally reinvent myself and be the person I felt I was inside. I could drop the masks, the acting, and be me. What a relief. Freedom! Such lightness followed as I explored my values and inner and outer worlds in a whole new way. I felt closer and more connected to myself initially, which was necessary after so many years of not knowing who I was or what I valued. I honoured my own space for around six years or so.

After the Rainbow Festival, I realised once more that I needed to connect with others, rebuild relationships, trust intimacy, and face my fears. As I became more connected and aware of me, I noticed people differently, too. I dropped the judgments (I'd been judgmental about both me and others). I invited strangers in and became very comfortable connecting with them. It was easier to love a stranger, and we always parted with a hug. I enjoyed the simplicity of loving a stranger and found it curious that I could feel such depth with a stranger and not with the people closest to me. I realised it was true when I connected with my heart and loved myself, warts and all. Only then could I accept and love others as they were. When I forgave myself and was kind to myself, then I could easily give this to others, too.

In 2013, I'd been working full time in my first 'real' professional job, trying to toe the line and be a 'good citizen'. In part, I think I did this trying to impress my ex-husband and my parents. I still hadn't fully accepted who I was and was still struggling internally between who everyone else thought I should be and who I knew I was deep down. Well, even deeper than that, I did not know how to be me. I had never seen 'me' before. I had no blueprint for me yet.

My ex-husband and I fleetingly revisited our relationship a second time around. Not long into it, he confessed about the affairs and shitty things he'd done. It was a weird moment as the counsellor part of me wanted to understand and empathise with him and accept that we both created our marriage. This was a symptom of the dysfunctionality we'd both participated in.

After he left that night, the rage that overtook me was years and years of toeing the line, of being the person everyone wanted me to be. I was angry at the lies, and suddenly every part of my life felt like a lie. I felt everything that had happened in my marriage, including the ending of it, was based on a different scenario.

Our marriage had become about disconnection, and I guess I was equally angry at myself for contributing. I was also angry at being so naïve, about taking care of his needs before mine in the aftermath of our separation. I was just angry. I threw pots and pans and plates, and two days later on the phone he said I should just forget about it and move on. No matter how hard I tried, my physical body and emotional body would not let me. The rage lasted for days, maybe even years later. I felt that not only had I been betrayed but also denied the right to feel the truth of our relationship.

One thing I was certain of in that moment was that my heart and intuition were always right. I recalled asking him during one of our counselling sessions eight years before if he was having an affair, and after hesitating, he denied it. As I reflected on this, I remembered this was when the dreams and nightmares had started. Perhaps they were preparing me for the future. I had so many conditions on what marriage and love should look like. I had given love and care to him throughout our whole marriage with a view to receiving it back. This is where all the rage and resentment were coming from. My love for him was fish love. It was about love that I needed or wanted in return, not true love. If you truly love something, you would want it to be free and be happy, to simply just love it, because it exists and is. I realised I never truly loved him. I was young and stuck in the old belief systems of fairy tales and fish love.

Most of all, I was angry at him for telling me eight years later. What was the point of that? The only way I could rationalise it was that the guilt within him had become too much, and he needed to rid himself of that. Two weeks later, we ended it for good. Three weeks after that, he had his future wife in his bed.

'Its easy standing in the crowd, but it takes courage to stand alone.'

MAHATMA GANDHI

Chapter 10
Nepal 2013 – Letting Go and Falling In

It was October 2013. My first time in Nepal, however my third time in Asia. I had been to Thailand, Cambodia and Malaysia, and I had felt a connection with Asia. Perhaps it was my Chinese/ Indo roots coming through, however Nepal was different, like the heart centre of it all.

My youngest son had a keen interest in culture and archaeological/ anthropological type things. I could see in his eyes when I was telling him about my trip that he wanted to come. So off we went and enjoyed three weeks in Nepal exploring.

The most spectacular and memorable part of the trip was doing the Ghorepani trek for five days. This is where I met Govinda for the first time. We were trekking through the Annapurna region and along the way we met up with other trekkers and their guides. It was on the first day, as we trekked up thousands of steps, that I first chatted and laughed with Govinda. At first I thought he was a lot older, until I learnt he was barely twentyone. Nepali people grow up faster it seems, and they learn about life at an early age. They're definitely not bubble wrapped as we are. The responsibilities they have and the hardship of life mean they understand cause and effect; and, most importantly, what it means to take responsibility for their own lives and the lives of their families and friends. From the moment they are born, they are being guided and raised by their family and communities. It is done in a way that is experiential and hands on, with a deep connection to their faith and the earth. They understand their relationship to everything and, most of all, each other. Their very survival depends on it.

After spending five days together, laughing, singing, talking about guitar, music and life, we really bonded. On the last night in Pokhara, saying goodbye, I was determined to stay in contact and promised him I'd be back. For some reason, my time there felt unfinished. I wasn't looking at him like a lover. Although, there was certainly an attraction, and I felt like I knew him despite our huge language barrier. My mind, with its practicality override button, pointed out all the reasons that it was a no-go zone, so I filed it under a nice experience and moved on.

Flying out of Nepal, I was grieving. That is the only way to explain it. I didn't know exactly what for. It was like my heart was being ripped away from its home. It was a strange experience, and I will never forget that feeling of 'missing' leaving Nepal that first time, like a piece of me was left behind. I vowed to help Govinda when the time was right, in whatever way I could. Nepali life was hard, and he was very poor.

I came back to my reality in Australia and realised with certainty, for the first time in my life, that I was truly trying to fit a round peg in a square hole. Honestly, my purpose was out there, not here in this cubicle nine to five every day. I was wasting my potential and my life. Nepal had given me a gift, although I still was not sure of the totality of it.

I left my job three months later and came back to my Phillip Island home. Phillip Island called me after my divorce six years earlier. I'd bought a lovely home there, which was perfect for about six years of healing and contemplation. It may have been the ocean and air, but nonetheless, it was my safe haven.

I decided that no matter how hard it was, I would no longer be a rolling stone. I was going to create my reality my way. I had found faith. I had started to uncloud my vision and felt more connected to self and the world than ever before. Although little did I know, I still had a fair amount of work to do. I wanted an income of $60,000 per year and hours that allowed flexibility and time for my family. I began manifesting.

I reconnected with my friend Nessa. She was working for an organisation as a trainer; mentoring, coaching and inspiring longterm unemployed people. She was loving it. I told her I wanted the contact details of the organisation. I wanted to get on board with this organisation. I was drawn to this job.

My vision had become clearer, and I knew this job would be a pathway to where I wanted to go. It would be the perfect apprenticeship and networking opportunity to create my longterm goal, which I might add, was still not one hundred per cent clear. I had finally started working with my heart; so I booked the $1,500 course in Training and Assessment in Melbourne, so I could be considered for the training role, having faith I would be employed by August that year.

As it happened, the universe likes to throw curve balls our way to test us. No sooner had I stepped into this heart space of faith, I lost my driver's licence. The Victorian authorities have a points system and with the amount of driving I did, up and down from Phillip Island to the Yarra Valley, I'd accumulated too many points. I was now unemployed, with no licence and living on Phillip Island one-and-a-half hours from the city. I had minimal opportunities, trying to maintain a mortgage and look after three children.

This became one of the lowest points of my life, and the day I had to ask my eldest son to borrow his savings was devastating.

I was completely destroyed; I felt stripped bare, vulnerable and broken. It was then my ex-husband tried for custody of our youngest daughter. I had no choice but to employ the services of a lawyer to defend this, quickly racking up a bill of $40,000 – not to mention the emotional strain on all of us. I was unravelling fast, and Nepal had become a distant memory.

It became harder to get out of bed. I found myself unwilling, stuck, and frustrated. If it wasn't for my sister, my mentor and friend Bob, and my eldest son, I'm not sure how I would have gotten through it. In a moment of fear, I took a job at the local supermarket, desperate for some income. On Phillip Island, it was difficult to find employment, as most businesses ran seasonally. This was a common complaint from many locals, and it was partly true.

When you live from the heart, you have to fully commit; you cannot have one foot in France and one foot in Italy. It does not work that way.

It was all in or all out. The job at the supermarket took time out of my day, limiting my time for creating. It was a long way from my vision for myself and definitely didn't inspire me. It was adding to my frustration and depression, despite the bit of income, which really wasn't much. It was a job taken out of fear, so how could it be in line with my heart or purpose? Which although it wasn't all clear yet, I knew I had to get that job with Bounce.

I quit the supermarket and started focusing on getting on board with Bounce. Bounce was a training organisation that focused on training long-term unemployed people. It helped them find their values and vision. Ironic really, because by now I'd become clear about my values and vision, I just needed to put it into action. However, the thing we need to learn is the thing we teach, right?

I emailed the CEO and after some discussion, she agreed to take me on, despite not having a course for me to teach yet. In the meantime, I could do some marketing for the business, earning me $500 per week. Finally, I got a break and was feeling like I had got back in alignment with my heart and purpose. I'd taken action alongside my values and the universe responded. As soon as I started with this organization, I felt valued, I felt on purpose. Everyone I met seemed to mirror back to me the parts of myself that I longed to unveil. Every colleague had something to teach, and I was a sponge, completely open and absorbing everything I could. I had so much gratitude for Bob, Nessa, and Mary at this time. They taught me to believe in the dream that anything was possible. I could co-create my reality.

Before long, I was working at Bounce as a trainer and for the first time in my life, felt completely balanced and aligned with my heart. I was on track. I was earning more money than I had ever earnt, doing a job I loved, hours I loved, and I was really good at my job.

I had received the confirmation and boost I needed to continue on this heart path. Training people every day, inspiring them to live their best heart life, I was receiving their success stories as well as my own. I was feeling more connected than ever. Watching people transform and realise their potential further fuelled my desire to fulfill mine, and I was growing fast. With all the mirrors in the room looking back at me, with all the light and dark in each of them, they were truly some of the best teachers I ever had.

After six months in this role, we had some upheaval with the contract, which brought up some fear again around stability in my role as a contractor. There was always that concern, so as I sat with the reality that I had no work for the next six weeks and no idea when the next course would be booked. It was time for the next creating session. This job was still reliant on government funding and other people. I did not like that part; I wanted to be the master of my creation. I had experienced disconnection and destruction; then creation, connection, contribution, and now, was back to the start again. Creation time.

I spent twelve months in an amazing role, facilitating learning exponentially. I became aware that in order for me to really expand and grow, not only my working goals but also my personal goals, that it was time to let go. Let go of all the feelings around being the perfect mother, about providing for my children and keeping the house, which had always felt like a noose around my neck. I reflected on my life and remembered my childhood dreams and my connection to the planet, contributing to things beyond my own personal gain. I always had this feeling. If I truly wanted to make a difference in the world and 'be the change' as Gandhi says, and show my children who I really am, then I needed to really start living it. Enough talk. I needed to take another step into uncertainty, trusting my heart, having faith and courage. I needed to listen to the quiet voice again, urging me to change things again.

Around this time, in court, my ex-husband declared I was unstable and was not fit to be my daughter's mother. He'd said I was unsettled, and this was not a good environment for her. I was devastated and really hurt by the accusations. The court did not entertain them at all and basically threw his case out, however the words were said out loud and were on repeat in my mind. I was suffering extreme mother guilt. I hated being thought of in that way. I was thinking, 'what else can you take from me?' I was feeling like an utter failure. Internally, I knew I wasn't being the mother that he, or most of the people I knew, thought I should be. The real me was still emerging. I was not confident about anything, and my self-esteem was shattered. I was, in short, questioning a lot of things.

On one level, I agreed he was better equipped at the time to be the stable parent. I was really struggling emotionally, and my life was spent travelling up and down the freeway to work. My daughter hardly saw me, as I struggled to pay the mortgage on my own and be the mother I wanted to be. It was battling these thoughts, and him, and that slowly chipped away at me, so I settled the court case. This resulted in a lump sum payment, and after costs, I had a small amount of savings. The money felt bittersweet after the ordeal and although it relieved the financial burdens and allowed me space to breathe; I felt it needed to be utilised in a way that transformed its energy.

'Life is a series of natural and spontaneous changes. Don't resist them; that only creates sorrow. Let reality be reality. Let things flow naturally forward in whatever way they like.'

LAO TZU.

Chapter 11
Kathmandu, Post Earthquake Day 4

I took a cab to the airport, hoping and praying that flights were operating as the phone lines were still pretty bad. There was no way of connecting with Govin once I was in the cab to the airport. He'd assured me we would meet in Pokhara, despite the fact he had no idea how he was getting there. He had declined my persistent offers for a plane ticket. It was clear at this stage that many tourists had already left the country, and here I was flying domestic to Pokhara, where my Nepali friends were.

On the way to the airport, I got my first real glimpse of the magnitude of the earthquake and its damage. In some ways, it was like driving through a war zone after a bomb attack and it was the images of the highway split in two that stayed in my mind. Such a bizarre image, one side was up two metres higher than the other side, almost like there had been earthworks in the area. The tar on the road looking like it was rubber and bent upwards, like the images of a surrealist painting.

I was now feeling a bit disturbed about leaving Govin, as he had insisted on catching a bus back to Pokhara. With what I'd seen on the way to the airport, I doubted the road to Pokhara would still be there. We had no way of contacting each other after I'd left him at the airport. There were no telecommunications, and this made me a little nervous, as I was in a foreign land, away from anyone I knew or trusted.

But it was my second glimpse into the generosity of the Nepali people. Sitting at the domestic terminal, I was alone for the first time in days and it hit me I was the only westerner in the airport. 'Was I crazy?' I asked myself. Yet as I turned inwards, I felt completely calm and the only place I wanted to be was back in Pokhara and with Govin.

I had no desire to go home. I did not feel unsafe and almost felt connected to the people somehow. I felt like if I left them, I'd be deserting them in their time of need. Even though I could do nothing to ease their concerns or stresses, I somehow felt my presence might be reassuring, that I was not leaving them in the midst of their country's devastation. Perhaps this was egotistical, I do not know, but I can honestly say I felt at peace and calmer than I'd ever felt in my life. Their efforts to connect with me seemed to make them smile, especially my attempts to speak their language.

The airspace became busy due to all the international airlines picking up all the tourists wanting to exit. On top of that were the Army helicopters and planes, so flights were delayed about five hours. I could feel the angst of the locals and their frustrations about not being able to get home to check on their loved ones. Despite this, I witnessed a graciousness, acceptance and patience among them. I finally arrived back at Pokhara at 3 p.m., six hours later.

I found out later that Govin had met with some friends and they got a ride out of the city on a truck. The road had become clogged with people wanting to get home to loved ones, and there were no buses available. He'd managed to find some friends travelling from Kathmandu, so together, they rode standing in the back of a truck on the crazy Nepali roads for nearly eleven hours. Jammed in like sardines and at times, they even rode on top of the truck, arriving in Pokhara at 3 a.m. Epic effort.

After reconnecting with my Nepali friends in Pokhara and checking everybody was safe and sound, I retreated to. By this time, I was sleeping through the tremors, albeit lightly, with an escape plan if needed. I had made peace with the idea that if it was my time, it was my time. To be honest, in this moment, I felt safe, even if it was the beginning of PTSD talking.

The next morning, it was clear to me! I could start a fund, raise money and use this situation to get more people aware of Nepal's plight. I am not sure where the idea came from, but as soon as I allowed it into my mind, it was underway. It felt right, and I noticed all the Nepali people staying in the guest house had their spirits lifted by my suggestion to start running missions. They all suddenly felt a little bit empowered. Like they had a purpose, something they could do. Together, we had a small meeting, and they were ready to run with whatever I suggested to help the victims. We put together a flyer and handed it out in the streets of Pokhara.

Suddenly, we had something we could do in a time of extreme powerlessness. I created an online GoFundme account and by the next day the fund had raised more than $1000. This excited my Nepali friends and so it was set in motion. This was our focus.

The word had got out through our flyers and by that evening, some tourists arrived. We asked them to sign up and share their skills and any funds they'd like to donate and asked them to come back to our first meeting the next day. The first meeting attracted thirty to forty people, all with a common goal to help in any way they could. Within forty-eight hours of arriving back in Pokhara, I was co-ordinating and leading a relief effort that was dedicated to helping villages in need of aid and support.

By the end of week one, we had assisted three villages with rice, tarps and basic needs. Soon, I had a small team around me, all assisting with their unique skills, and for the first time in my life, I felt connected, on purpose, centred and present. People were donating from all over the world. In particular, a few tourists stood out to me as being very committed, so I invited them to play key roles and delegated some of the tasks to them. This soon became the core group, which included six Nepali friends, two

Americans, one Canadian, two French, and me. We were all using our networks to promote and share the relief effort and together we really created something. It was amazing. In Pokhara the town was abuzz with collection points, groups coming together to support Nepali villages. It was inspiring to be a part of it, and I was in awe of the generosity and trust shown by foreigners and locals. Within three months, we had raised and spent a total of $45,000-50,000AUD and assisted thirteen villages – approximately 11,000-15,000 people.

I really found my flow. I was so present, so in my element, nothing bothered me. I didn't feel like anything was missing in my life at all. I felt supported and at complete peace within. Like I was one hundred per cent on purpose, completely aligned with my dharma.

Australian dollars go so much further here. For example, a thirty-kilogram bag of rice costs 1200 rupee, approximately $15.00AUD, could feed a small family for a month or more.

dollars and we were feeding and assisting thousands of people. Suddenly, the idea of spending thousands on a mortgage and bills in Australia seemed futile and purposeless. I felt like my money and my time could be so much more useful and worthwhile here. It just made sense, more sense than anything in my life. For the first time, I felt like what I was doing was actually making a direct difference to the lives of people. It felt like the most natural and on purpose thing in the world. My heart was filled with so much gratitude from all the generosity, from all the support, near and far. I was energised and my mind was quiet!

I was aligned with my values for the first time – conscious, connected, creative, contribution. It was like everything suddenly made sense. Everything I'd ever experienced had culminated to this exact point in time, to be available to me at this moment for me to step into this role. I felt like I was where I was supposed to be. Govin and I were busy doing the aid work and focused on helping people in villages and making a difference. We were inseparable, and it felt natural, like I had found the other half of me. I was in awe of him. I came to appreciate his wisdom, knowledge, and maturity. Here was this man who grew up in a house with no power, no toilet, bathroom or hot water, sometimes going without dinner, giving his heart and time to help others in need. A far cry from the individualised capitalist drive that existed in Australian life. Forgetting about all his own problems to help others. There was something about him that really connected to my heart, giving me perspective on what was important in life. Material possessions suddenly held no appeal. Slowly, we became close. I had consciously made the decision to open my heart, not judge, not question, and to have no expectations. How could I expect anything from a young Nepali man? So many cultural differences, there was no framework here! A whole new world to explore for me. An opportunity to face my fears, through love.

I decided that if I did not open my heart and be prepared to have it broken, then I could never experience love again. This relationship was the perfect training ground for me to deal with my fears about expectations. Love is a whole thing. You cannot have it in halves. You cannot decide to just dip your toe in. You have to either be all in, or you are living in fear and that is not love. So, for the first time in my life, I did not think about practical things – age differences, cultural differences, responsibilities, or being rejected. I just jumped into the deep end of the swimming pool, having faith and knowing I could swim, to just honour the feeling and the soul connection that was undoubtable.

I told him I expected nothing in return, however I loved him so deeply I just wanted to be allowed to love him. He did not say much, and for me, it was perfect to just sit in that space of loving without needing anything back.

*'The peace of god is with them whose mind and soul
is in harmony, who are free from desire and wrath,
who know their own soul.'*

BHAGAVAD GITA.

Chapter 12
Growing

To evolve is to grow, is to integrate, to expand and sometimes contract. To evolve is to move with and flex with, to move through and beyond. To evolve all aspects of self within a lifetime is a huge task, whether done consciously or not, evolution happens in its own time based on the triggers, challenges and environmental pressures that surround us. Evolution or change is indefinite and constant. There is no timeline and certainly no expectation of how, what, or when. Everything and everyone is in a constant state of flexing, bending, growing, expanding, contracting and moving. Nothing is stationary. We are in constant relationship with everything, constantly communicating sub-consciously and consciously. To be stationary is to be devoid of life, stale and slowly dying. How we evolve is a unique blend of our own perceptions, sub-consciousness, and the environment around us. How we perceive our journey on earth plays a major role in how we transform any information that comes to affect our state of being. The universe works in harmony with us, what we think we become. Everything we encounter we are in co-creation with; simultaneously with the universe; subconsciously and consciously by our actions and reactions. Sometimes we expand and sometimes we contract, like a muscle does when we work out.

When a woman gets pregnant, she is on a creative journey. She is creating a being within her and this being is also creating itself, responding and growing within the environment that it is in. After growing through each of the stages of the pregnancy, the small baby eventually outgrows its environment and, through discomfort and uncomfortable contractions, it has no choice but to leave its safe haven and move out into the new world. Think about that process for a moment and really look at how it parallels our lives every day. We are being prepared for change and growth from the moment we are conceived. To go against this is to go against nature and life. Life is all about cycles, growth, expansion and contraction, depression, and creation are just this.

How we grow and change depends on how much effort or consciousness we choose to have whilst taking action, or where we choose to focus our attention.

Think for a moment about a plant, how it grows and how it depends on its environment and the interaction it may have with other plants, animals or humans. No two plants are the same. Each one slightly different, different shapes, the amount of leaves or branches varies and the height and location too. Just like no two people are ever the same, even if created by the same two parents, even twins are not the same one hundred per cent.

When we become connected with nature, then we are guided everywhere. It shows us where we are all the time. Like a map or inner compass. In winter, everything is dying or sleeping. Resting, knowing that soon it will become spring, and new growth emerges, bringing light, colour, new creations. Every year, this cycle happens. Night always becomes day, just like every contraction happened before every expansion. Suffering exists in the resistance to it, resistance to the inevitable change or influence. If we connect and work with nature, then we can only ever evolve, lovingly with purpose and vision. Nature knows that it is here to grow and expand and it just gets on with it. It will always consciously fill the spaces. In actuality, if we want to survive as a human being, our best chance is to work with nature, not against it. Water always flows into the spaces, as does air. Fire follows the oxygen/air and dust, and dirt particles will fly with the wind and create new mountains. It's all linked, working in harmony.

When the earthquake happened in Nepal, we were reminded of this. The earth is still forming, changing, responding and growing, adapting to the environment. Nothing is still. I recall a Nepali person saying to me, 'this is an opportunity for Nepal to create'.

'Wow', I thought. They were already focusing on creation from the depths of destruction. This is a human quality that was evident after the Thailand tsunami as well. It was noted that people who have less and grow in an undeveloped part of the world are often more resilient and can cope better with the trials of life. I think that is lacking in Western society.

The people I had met so far on my journey had become significant people in my life for so many reasons. They all inspired me, for their dedication, commitment and focus for the cause, and this further motivated me. Complete destruction of the old and creation of the new. So, I needed an earthquake to move, to let go and step into myself. Taureans are stubborn, but really, an earthquake? Being an earth sign I guess it makes sense, so here I was, thrust into that relationship with nature, grounded and present. My time in Nepal had only just begun. It was the start of something bigger, and although I was not quite sure where or what it was, I knew I had to stay indefinitely to complete this cycle of learning. I did not feel I could leave yet amid such destruction and profound unravelling. I was also being shaken to my core.

I went back to Australia in June 2015 after I'd been busy and fully absorbed in relief work for two months. I was back in Australia for three weeks to pack up my old life and relocate to Nepal to continue on this mission. I went home feeling so much clarity and centeredness that it was easy packing up my house, manifesting a tenant and tying up loose ends, raising much needed funds and heading back to Nepal.

I was committed to long-term change, not only within myself but also working and contributing to projects that would help people. I wanted to work in a person centred way that preserved and empowered Nepali people to rebuild their lives and protected their culture and way of life. Despite the obvious judgments and reservations of some of my family and friends about me leaving my Australian life, I decided that as long as I stayed in my heart centre and trusted it, they would eventually see me and accept me. I had faith. Needless to say, the night my eldest son gave a speech at a small gathering for me, I was absolutely certain I was doing the right thing. I was moved to tears by the wisdom and compassion in his words. That ultimately gave me the last bit of courage to take that last step and leave Australia and all my possessions.

By the time I left, the only things I still owned were my car, laptop, guitar, some clothes, and a few sentimental items. For the first time, I felt free and my mother's guilt was gone.

There was no room for fear, as my heart was filled with love and connectedness, and I was contributing to something greater than myself.

'There are waves and there is the wind, seen and unseen forces. Everyone has these same elements in their lives, the seen and unseen: Karma and Free Will.
The question is "how are you going to handle what you have?' You are riding the karmic wave underneath and the wind can shift. Everyone must take what they see and deal with, that which is unseen."

KUAN YIN

Chapter 13
Monsoon

As Goddess Kali ensures, there is always balance. She does not allow us to be led astray, as she keeps us always aligned through the cycle of change. One of the few consistent things that exists in the universe is movement and change. Love comes in many forms, especially through destruction. Kali is the goddess of the shadows.

The first mission I physically went on affected me the most – it was when I met the village women. Until this point, I had met some Nepali women from Govin's family and at a local wedding, but never in their village as a stranger. This was a humbling and privileged moment I will never forget. The women in Harrabot village were all uneducated, living a very traditional village life looking after the farm and children. Except one woman. She had been living for a while overseas and upon marrying her husband had to return with him to his village, as was the Nepali village custom. Her role now was to look after the family. She could speak some English, so she became the interpreter as I sat and chatted to the locals about their situation.

It had taken us about five hours to get the bus loaded with aid up to the village of Harrabot, a small village near Lamjung in the central region of Nepal. This was an eye-opening experience on just how challenging the terrain was in Nepal. The bus was loaded up in Pokhara that morning and it was full. Driving up to Harrabot with a loaded bus was hair-raising. As it straddled on two to three wheels, I held my breath a few times. I soon focused on the skill level of the driver and his ability to drive a passenger bus that was at least a fifty-year-old recycled rickety bus from India. The logistics of getting aid and help into villages were going to be tough.

We were notified by our contacts that this particular village was being overlooked. Once there, we witnessed the UN aid trucks whizzing past, taking aid further up the mountain to the larger villages. Perhaps there were more people in need higher up the mountain? Although I later learned that the aid often went to the higher caste people or people with political power in Nepal over the true needy.

It was meeting these people that cemented within me the importance of all life and that numbers should have nothing to do with it. Person centred means person to person, humanitarian, what it is to be human. Every 'one' person is as important as another. Hence, we called our group 'people helping people'. It was here I sat chatting with the women in my broken Nepali and learnt of the struggle of daily life in Nepali villages, with or without the earthquake. They have learnt to live with it, accept it, and they all seemed to have this amazing sense of 'we are all in this together'. They were connected as a people, to the land and each other, and it was here that I too felt really connected to Nepal and its people.

The old woman told stories of the earthquake and how it was really difficult because in their village many of the men were away overseas working and could not come home to help them rebuild. This was common in Nepal, as they often had their passports removed upon arrival in the Arabic countries as part of their work contract. Or they'd taken out huge mortgages to go abroad and could not afford to come home to their families. I couldn't help but notice there was one old man left in the village who was disabled with the loss of his legs. His family kept asking us for extra things because of his situation, with tears in our eyes. Of course, we gave all we could give in that moment.

The old woman wanted to share details of angry gods and spirits that caused the earthquake. She was concerned that they were still unhappy and was scared to sleep at night in case they came again. Her eyes were full of fear and her voice had a hint of hysteria, repeating over and over the noise of the quake as she recalled it.

I remembered learning that Govin's mother also believed in these spirits and gods and conducted her daily life trying to appease them. One day, she even asked me if we had a moon in Australia. It was in that moment I realised we cannot force evolution; we cannot force a mind to expand. It will happen naturally based on the environment and experiences that are shaping it. It is important as modern citizens of the developed world that we do not impose our educated minds upon first peoples and undeveloped nations faster than they ask for it. Instead, it is our duty to learn from them. The younger women were less superstitious and more practical. They were worried about their farms because they could not rebuild and tend to the farm at the same time. They were worried about the winter coming; that the children would go hungry because some of the animals were killed in the earthquake and the crops were not doing well.

I witnessed just how strong these Nepali women were; they were often the backbone of their communities. Govin had said to me many times they were the back wheel of the motorcycle, the power. If the women in the village could not do their job, the communities and strong family units would collapse. The women ran the farms and the homes and looked after the children. In this culture, without them, families would not function. They truly are the strength. I could see the goddess Kali in them all, and it was after this experience in Harrabot that I truly felt a sense of responsibility to be a voice for these people.

In the coming months, we assisted many villages and packed many jeeps, trucks, buses, and even donkeys.

We took aid into Gorkha region, the epicentre of the quake, and this certainly tested our logistic skills. Thankfully, we had two ex-Army men amongst us and with their help we could coordinate aid to a remote village that took two days' trekking with donkeys to get there. Later, this same village was part of a school rebuild project that was facilitated by our group 'People Helping People'.

On another journey, we packed rice into 1.5-kilogram bags and carted over thirty bags into trucks. We delivered the goods to the nearest village by road and the locals walked the threehour trek down the mountain to pick up their goods. Then to see people trek the three hour-long walk back up the mountains to their homes, or what was left of them, was hard – sometimes with thirty kilogram rice bags and babies on their backs. These people humbled me in ways I cannot describe.

We visited so many damaged villages we became a little numb to the devastation and just got on with the job. I think it was a way to help and deal with our guilt over the fact we could go home at any time. These were their homes, though, destroyed. With tarps and mats on the ground, this was the best we could do for now, as it was emergency relief only.

With their houses in rubble all around them, each time we visited, I felt myself becoming more aware of the long road to recovery for Nepal. If it were even possible. Nepal was already significantly below the poverty line. With no industry and no export, how could they recover with a government ill-equipped to deal with such events? I was looking at things differently. Every journey was a significant learning experience in so many ways, from logistics, to co-ordination, to networking, and political navigation and structure in Nepal. In a different world, working in a different culture requires so many creative and sometimes risk-taking methods to get the job done.

Monsoon set in around August and Pokhara had become a ghost town. No tourists were left. My crew had all gone back to their lives in Europe and America. Funds had stopped rolling in and people around the world had new disasters to focus on. Businesses were closing, being pulled down, or renovated. Lots of people were wandering around not knowing what to do, because business was so slow. A town that was usually abuzz with tourists was quiet. The locals were getting worried about how to stay afloat if the tourists didn't return. This was a lesson in acceptance and patience. Monsoon had made aid work even more dangerous this year, because the earthquake had loosened land everywhere. In a country already susceptible to landslides, villages were now on high alert for the second phase of the disaster.

Although Pokhara wasn't really affected by the earthquake, its ripple effect had affected everyone in Nepal. Nepalis' number one income source was tourism. Businesses were undoubtedly impacted and that meant families were as well. Many people work in businesses to feed and support not only their immediate families, but their extended families as well, and in some cases half a village.

The hardest thing at that point was wanting and needing to get out into the field, yet I was stuck waiting. A massive lesson in recognising that there is no 'fixing', there is only ever imperfection in perfection and vice versa. A time to be, reflect and accept reality. It was monsoon time. Things had changed. Kali had now released the landslides, and water issues were affecting all the people who could not rebuild yet, which was the majority. When it rains in Nepal, it pours. The roads had become rivers and the thunder and lightning were like nothing I had ever heard or seen. The noise rippled and rolled across the valleys, and it was extremely frightening. I could, in these moments, understand why the villagers were superstitious and believed the gods must be angry.

There was something about monsoon time that forced me to stop, reflect, and re-evaluate my reasons and motivations. It forced me to slow down even more. For someone like me, being from Melbourne, Australia, this was not easy. We are so used to being busy, and on a schedule, and our air-conditioned and heated cars enabled us to avoid the weather a little and keep our daily routines intact.

The government in Nepal allows children up to thirty-three days off school in monsoon. It is easy to understand why. The roads become impossible and if you live in villages and have no choice but to walk to school and the rain starts, it can be a dangerous journey home. Trekking through the Himalayan mountains trying to avoid sliding down the mountain or worse still, being caught in a landslide or temporary raging river torrent was a priority. This was a forced meditation by the universe on my part and as I struggled, resisted and got more frustrated by not being able to do 'something'. I slowly learned about acceptance and grace. Nepal was now teaching me patience, and how to 'be' in the midst of chaos. I was learning once again.

Govin and I spent more time together in a whole new way. In the previous months, we had been so busy supporting each other through the earthquake and relief effort that we both witnessed each other in many situations. He could calm and centre me with just a few words, like a knife cutting through butter. He has since told me he was equally in awe of me and I think that somewhere during this time, we fell in love.

We moved in together in a flat in Pokhara. During this time of 'being', I focused on raising more money and supporting and mentoring local Nepali relief groups. The occasional workshop at the university encouraged the youth to think creatively and take action towards their dreams. Every day we would practice guitar, sing, and I started to write. I've always enjoyed writing, however often felt I didn't have the space to do so. Now I was given the space, and it just flowed. I started blogging about Nepal and slowly processed the experiences through writing.

It was during this time we revisited Govin's desire to go to Australia. He had a dream of going there and fixing his 'family problem', as he called it. He wanted to build his family a muchneeded home. This was one thing I loved about him. Even though his family was poor and had nothing, he gave everything to help others in their time of need during the relief effort. He would tell me stories of his life and I felt these stories had not been told before. Sometimes holding back tears, I listened for hours as we chatted about life, Hindu culture, and the world. I wanted to help him achieve his lifelong dream. We'd discussed the best way to be together, and also achieve our dreams. Getting married seemed the most logical thing to do.

For me, the marriage idea was just a formality to make it possible for him to come to Australia. I knew this would give him the freedom he wanted. Few people are aware the world rates passports based on a set of criteria, which values a human based on his culture, financial status, and religion. Nepali passports are considerably low on the list and because of this, they cannot get visas to many affluent countries. So even an ambitious Nepali with money essentially may not leave his country without some creative effort, and if they are over thirty, virtually impossible. For those under thirty, a student visa was the best way. However, a score of at least seven in English was required, but difficult to attain.

I loved Govin more than I had ever loved any man. So, for the first time in my life, despite reservations about what a marriage would look like with him, I decided once again to have no expectations and go with the flow. I knew without doubt I could at least love him, support him, and provide him with an opportunity to change the fate of his family.

In the following months, Govin and Nepal taught me so much about what marriage was about. I found the part of myself that deeply wanted to be connected and in complete unity with another. It had been buried deep inside when I had given up on the fairy tale. My old ideas of marriage were so dysfunctional and now I had a second chance to revisit marriage in a whole new light. Around the middle of the monsoon season, when all was quiet, we booked a short holiday to Cambodia to celebrate and take some time out. Govin had never been outside Nepal, and I wanted to show him the ocean. After trawling the internet for countries that Nepali citizens could visit with minimal visa requirements, we found Cambodia. Govin was extremely nervous about travelling out of his country in this way and somewhat felt undeserving. I assured him he deserved it after the past few months, and it would be a good way for us to get to know each other a little better, in a different, neutral environment.

He loved to swim, so I knew it would be an amazing time for him and for me. The joy of sharing this experience with him was a blessing for sure.

Cambodia is an interesting place full of history, culture, and mystery. I had visited once before, although I didn't get to the coast. I was looking forward to going back this time with Govin. Cambodia has a rich and colourful history and, more recently, a sad one. The amazing Hindu and Buddhist temples are so ancient, mystical, and steeped in stories of another dimension of time that your mind wanders off into some far-off place; contemplating the way it all looked before the jungles and monkeys reclaimed them. The temples are all set deep in the jungle and in some cases, the jungle is deep within the temples – another example that nature is always rearranging itself to adapt to its environment and obstacles.

Govin and I set off on our two-to-three-week journey to Cambodia, flying out of Kathmandu. However, going through customs, we had an ugly experience with one of the customs officials. He questioned Govin and refusing to stamp his exit on the passport (an example of the ignorance and caste system in Nepal). The official was asking him if he had money and if he could afford to leave; he did not trust that we were together and was extremely rude and derogatory towards him. This made me so angry. I was quite direct with the customs man, demanding he speak English so I could understand, as I knew he was trying to bamboozle Govin and prey on his naivety. Eventually, another customs official stepped in, and after some discussion with me assuring that I was with Govin and supporting him, he let us through.

The plane ride was surreal. Govin had only been on a small ten-seater flight between Pokhara and Kathmandu at this point and this time, he was on a jet that seated approximately four hundred people. We arrived in Siem Reap after the five-hour flight and Govin was extremely quiet, just taking it all in.

In the morning, we took a taxi to Siem Reap's temple sanctuary and got taken on a tuk tuk around all the temples, including Angkor Wat. This was a massive day, and once again, Govin was awestruck by everything. He noticed the temple carvings and monuments had similarities to his Hindu gods in Nepal; often saying that they were the same, but with small differences.

Later, we heard stories of kings who had conquered or visited these areas influencing the faith of that time, weaving Hindu and Buddhism into their own unique faith. It lay buried for hundreds of years in the jungle, untouched until recent times. Once again, I am in awe of how much we can learn from ancient cultures and stories.

After a couple of days in Siem Reap, we headed south to Sihanoukville to visit the coastal region. I had never been to this area, so I was keen to visit. I had missed the ocean living in Nepal, surrounded by mountains, and this would be Govin's first time to see it. I was a wee bit excited. The long twelve-hour bus ride was a cool way to see the landscape and village life. It was air-conditioned, so I was happy, as it was so hot and humid in Cambodia that it was difficult to not work up a sweat just from breathing. I was reminded of how flat Cambodia was and the amount of water in lakes and rivers. For these people, fishing was a way of life. Govin mentioned the similarities to villages in Nepal, and he found this intriguing.

During the trip, I realised just how intuitive and deeply connected Govin was. We were out touring in the searing Cambodian humidity, and he told me he felt the smiles of the Cambodian people were not real. He felt they were hiding their pain with their smiles. I shared the recent sad history of the Cambodian people. He did not know that in the 1970s, Cambodia had suffered mass genocide under Pol Pot. However, once I shared the story, he understood what he was feeling around these people, a sense of loss, not only of their relatives and significant loved ones, but of culture and knowledge, too.

In Cambodia, it was a joy for me to watch Govin experience this fascinating place. He was a long way outside of his comfort zone. He had started to understand the difficulties of not having the language and was reliant on me a little more than usual due to the language barrier in Cambodia. Govin noted it must have been challenging for me in Nepal not having Nepalese, and at this point we decided he would help me learn more Nepalese.

Govin was surprised the Cambodians' English was not as good as his. He was equally surprised they seemed a bit behind in their personal development, despite the physical development that was going on in their cities. I think the experience really helped his confidence and believing in himself that he could leave Nepal and go to Australia.

For me, it was clear the Americans had made a big impact in Cambodia, and was destined to become westernised fast. Despite the lack of quality education, there were a lot of expats doing business, and the cities really felt very westernised. A lot had changed since my last visit in 2011.

Govin was in awe of seeing the ocean. I guess he never thought he'd see or touch the ocean, living in Nepal, a landlocked country. We caught a boat over to Koh Rong Island with plans to stay in a beautiful cabin on the beach. It had seemed like a lovely idea at the time. However, upon arrival we learnt the usual ferryboat to the cabin did not operate at this time of year, so we would have to trek forty-five minutes through the jungle to our cabin! This time still makes me laugh. I was in my element, I love an adventure. Poor Govin was fearing for his life, I am sure of it. Here he was in a strange land, a strange country, with a foreign language, and we had to trek through a jungle with no map, to sleep by a wild ocean that could swallow him whole. It was a strange day indeed, and we were tired after a long bus journey from Siem Reap. I walked it barefoot, as I only had thongs on, and the rain had started. That meant slippery thongs. I chose to embrace the adventure of it. The feeling of walking barefoot through the jungle in the humidity with the summer rain was really something special. Govin quietly trekked behind me, probably thinking I'd lost my mind.

I laughed inside, contemplating all the crazy thoughts he might have about this unlikely experience.

Upon arrival, we were so surprised at the seclusion of this place. There was hardly anyone on this side of the island as it opened out into the wide, expansive ocean. The waves were so big; we didn't dare go into the water. Apparently there had been a cyclone off Japan, which was creating this massive swell. It was a restless night for Govin. He kept feeling like the waves were going to come and wash our small cabin away – it literally sat just metres from the water's edge, surrounded by jungle. We trekked back to the other side again. It was so strange to me how uneasy he felt here. To me it was paradise, for him it was a strange, alien land. It really brought home the isolated life he had led in Nepal, a landlocked country that, until forty years ago or so, was traversed only on foot.

Chapter 14
Tiger Land

Returning to Nepal, I think Govin was relieved to have both feet on the ground again. We headed straight for Baglung (Baglung translates to Tiger land), Govin's family home. Baglung gets its name from the many tigers that used to live in the area.

Baglung is a beautiful place high on a big flat rock overlooked by Dhaulagiri and Nilgiri mountains, part of the Annapurna Sanctuary. Two rivers run on either side of it, one of which is the Kali Gandaki River. Baglung is famous for its rich king, and temple dedicated to the Goddess Kali. Although there is no monarchy left in Nepal after the assassination of the last king back in 2001, except for the Last Kingdom in the Upper Mustang.

Nepal has only in the last few years or so, established a government after being under military rule. I couldn't help but notice that they released the first Nepalese constitution just three months after the 2015 Earthquakes. Needless to say, I think it might still be in debate and the cause of the usual political issues that keep the country from developing.

The history of Baglung has been recorded from around the 16th century. King Pratap Narayan of Galkot married the Princess of Palpa. The king brought a statue of the goddess Kali along with him as a dowry. Legend follows that nobody could carry the sword of Kali. One day, a youth from the Kunwar Chhetri family came and tried to carry the sword. To everyone's surprise, this unassuming young man could do it. He could carry the sword. He was the chosen one and given the honorary title of Khadka ('khadga' meaning the sword). One night, when the wedding procession reached where Baglung is today, the king had a dream. In his dream, goddess Kali said she liked the place and wished to stay there. The king then built a temple in honour of goddess Kali and designated the Khadka as caretaker.

To this day, the Baglung temple is one of the most beautiful temples, surrounded in a natural shaded forest.

I needed to reacquaint myself with Kali and to reconnect with Nepal, so for me, this was the place. Sitting up high on the hill, looking out across the valleys with its winding rushing Kali River, I felt quite at peace as I chatted to Govin about all sorts of things, including our future.

'This is the river they take the dead to. I have seen many dead bodies here', Govin informed me. Close relatives and friends carry them down the steep descent on bamboo rafts to be burned.

There is a Hindu ritual performed and the son of the deceased must shave his head. The family cannot be touched for about seven to eleven days. They cannot eat anything but rice, and no salt. It is a ritual and practice that has not been questioned or altered for thousands of years. Every villager that dies near this river is brought here, even if they must trek for days. Years later, I would witness a funeral here, an old grandmother meeting her end with hundreds of locals gathered to witness her burning and crossing into the afterlife.

Yet despite its association with the dead, I found the river somewhat soothing. The loud rush of its water cleansing as it washed away any trace of negativity, always renewing and sustaining life. The river is part of everyday life in Nepal; it is the place they wash, catch fish, meet at, swim in, and lastly, burn the dead.

Govin also shared with me it was a Hindu belief, until recent times, that the wives of deceased men should also be burned alive with their husband's corpses. It was a last act of devotion to continue to serve and respect their husbands in the next life. Nepali believe that when you marry, you are married for seven lifetimes. He explained that this was a belief that was related to an ancient story about Goddess Parvati and the God Shiva. Later, I watched a movie about this very custom and it was quite a devastating concept for me to digest. But it certainly highlighted the power of an extremely patriarchal interpretation of the Hindu scriptures at that time.

Whilst watching the river and acknowledging all that it had witnessed, I was aware of the amazing qualities of the rushing waters. Rivers are the life source of the planet, like the arteries that carry blood. The circle of life operating beautifully. The river is in perfect balance as the river is life and takes life. A perfect representation of Kali always balancing creation and destruction, life and death. However, even though I had this realisation, I could not help but shed a tear for all the lives lost at the hand of this powerful river – women, children and men – as part of their daily lives here in Nepal. Whilst acknowledging, without these powerful rivers, there would be no life here at all.

In Nepal, every major region used to have its own king. Proudly, the kings would have palaces and rule the surrounding villages. These kings would often war with each other, and over time, the kings were defeated by the mighty Gorkha King, the last king of Nepal. I couldn't help but notice that Gorkha was at the epicentre of the earthquake.

After spending time in beautiful Baglung, exploring the town and some nearby motorbike drives up the mountain, I felt quite at home there. Despite life appearing simple here, it is equally hard for many. When I observed Govin's family at home, I could see this, however they seemed reasonably happy and content with their daily routines.

People here are so busy surviving that there is no time for the complicated mental tasks we undertake in the developed world.

It seems there is little need for women to go to school when this is the life they have, as they have too much to do in the home. However, for the country to develop and to help women in the future as cities expand, we need to help them get educated in ways that work in their communities. More women are being educated in the city areas, but there is a long way to go.

Govin's family has very little, and even now I find it difficult to understand how they lived that way. A small home of just four rooms, his mother slept in the kitchen room. They had to fetch their water, cook over small fires, and grow all their own food. However, I can't help but feel that despite the hard work, there is a beauty and peacefulness in the simplicity of living in a community like this. People find joy in the smallest things and walking everywhere is a way of life. Govin was blessed that he could get a good education and perhaps that, combined with the internet coming to Nepal, meant he was given an opportunity to change his family's future.

As with the Aboriginals of Australia, the Native Americans and other tribal cultures of the world, it is imperative that we learn from, preserve, support, and protect these cultures. There is so much to learn about, like how to live in harmony with our planet in a connected way. I believe these people who live off the land in a simple way hold the key to our future. Through their stories, legends, and myths, we can find our way back to a simpler, harmonious way of being. We are not separate from nature, we are nature.

I have seen this in Nepal and with my Nepalese family. They understand, accept, and work with nature, never resisting it. It is a different way of being, and I am learning so much being part of it. Ancient knowledge is interwoven into their lives in such a way that at times it keeps them safe and guided, and sometimes it limits them. I am now studying Ayurveda, an Ancient Vedic Medicine/science, similar to Traditional Chinese Medicine, so that I can have a better understanding of this and do what I can to assist in the preservation of ancient knowledge that serves all of humanity harmoniously with nature.

Monsoon time in Nepal seemed to go on forever. Nepali life almost stops. Nepali people are good at 'being'. It seems for most of the year, the Nepali people wear open shoes. It is interesting for an Aussie chick, being here in the monsoon, as it's always hot and humid. You cannot escape it. In comparison, at my home in Melbourne, Victoria, in the south of Australia, the winter is long, cold and wet. I never realised how much the environment can affect you. I started to understand how the weather and the environment played such a key role in the way I lived. My energy levels and state of mind were more closely linked to the weather and environment than I ever thought possible.

Some days, I would stroll along Fewa Taal in Pokhara (the lake), and I would find myself willing it to rain as I watched the sky. I would sit looking across the beautiful lake and I could not help but wonder if the purpose of the Monsoon was to create gratitude and humbleness. There is something about the magnitude of the wild sky grumbling, growling, rolling, and rumbling before she opens up her skies and the rain falls. It was seeing nature in all her rawness and power, surrendering, and accepting. Those rains were cleansing the Nepali landscape, clearing the air, and washing away all the dust and dirt. I learnt to love the rain there.

So different from my feelings of frustration and depressed energy that I'd often felt in Melbourne when it rained. In Nepal, it was experienced differently. I remember as she was building those grey clouds, the humidity rose to such a level that the air was so wet and sticky you could not escape it. By the time the sky opened up, I was willing to stand there and have a shower under those big black clouds.

The rain was heavy, creating rivers with its volume, so it was not too hard to understand why the roads here are so badly damaged and somewhat temporary in places. The water was filling up tanks, rice paddies. Rivers were rushing so hard, so fast and so big, that it was wild and dangerous just to be nearby. Landslides were a real threat here. I If you were living in the mountains, it was a part of your life. You could honestly wake up one morning to find half your village gone. Sadly, this became a reality for a village on the route to Baglung. One morning, my friend messaged me urgently asking for help. Overnight the rain had come down so hard that a water tank, which had its foundations loosened during the earthquake, shifted and created a landslide. Unbeknown to the village it serviced below, it slid then tipped on top of the hill, bringing with it a landslide, which took out five family homes and killed thirty-five people. It was devastating. What could we do? We felt powerless. I got up and checked our supplies. We had ten sleeping bags, medical supplies, some food, soap, and supplies. I donated $1000 from our funds and we took a bus out to the village about one hour from Pokhara. We had no idea what to expect.

Upon arrival, I was aware of the sadness in the village. Like most villages here, families are all connected and the communities themselves are like extended families. The story that seemed to stand out and affect us all was the poor pregnant woman who went to visit her friend for the evening and never returned home. She was crushed by the mud alongside her friends in their home.

As I went for a walk into the village, it was with mixed emotions I walked on the very land where people lay buried under layers of mud and silt, and broken homes. Seeing the broken household goods, kid's shoes and blankets, buckets, and other random items, I had to disconnect just to be there. The sadness and devastation was a lot to take in. Knowing that beneath the soil lay somebody's, mother, father, child, cousin. The energy, of course, was extremely sombre, and again I was reminded about the importance of every life. We have a responsibility as humans to recognise that every life is valuable and worthy. It is hard to explain exactly the feeling and what I saw here that day as we were led through the damage and devastation by a local man.

There were tears and there was silence, as we stood powerless with nothing else but our little bit of aid. I really felt for the people in Nepal in this moment, as I witnessed their acceptance of such tragedies as part of Nepali life. The terrain here is still very wild and untamed. There is no certainty of anything.

As I descended the side of the hill, I met an old lady carrying her donations and she looked at me intently, saying, 'dhanyabad' (thank you in Nepali). She started telling me in Nepali about losing her daughter and future grandchild. What could I do but be silent and cry tears with her? It was an experience I shall never forget, humbling me and reminding me about the fragility of life and the importance of living a loving and connected life; breathing every moment as we are not in control of when it is our time to part this existence.

In that moment, nothing mattered to me. Money, things, anything of material value seemed utterly irrelevant, and all I wanted to do was scream at the whole world to stop chasing money and take notice of reality and help one another. There is enough for everyone. I wanted to see more contribution happening to make the lives of these people better. I wanted the world to take more responsibility. Travelling back to Pokhara, I cried silent tears and vowed to continue on my journey towards a life in service of others in some way.

Chapter 15
Culture, Language and Learning

In a culture and place so vastly different to Australia, a constant jolt to the senses, Nepal was always asking me to step out of my comfort zone. To step out of my head and into my heart. To not judge and just allow. To be the observer. Acceptance and patience became my mantra here. Govin was forever saying bistaari bistaari (slowly, slowly). Every day I practiced a little more Nepali language and every day I learned more about Hinduism and the Nepali culture. It is a mixture and blend of Hindu, Buddhist and Shamanic practice that goes back over 6,000 years of traditions and experiences. I looked up the definition of Hinduism. This is what I found; 'Hinduism is not just a faith. It is the union of reason and intuition that cannot be defined, but is only to be experienced. Evil and error are not ultimate. There is no hell for that means there is only a place where God is not, and there are sins which exceed his love'.

Reading this unknown quote explaining Hinduism was like coming home. It resonated with me so deeply, like I had known it for a millennium. I had lived with this thought for most of my life, without having the words to express it. Never having a frame of reference or understanding of why I thought this way. There were so many things, signposts and synchronicities flowing through my world confirming this experience for me every day in Nepal. I truly felt connected to some ancient wisdom from the past guiding me along.

Many people are unaware that many spiritual and religious practices have evolved from the Vedas, which is where Hinduism developed, and after this came Buddhism. They cannot say exactly how, as it is difficult to track how it evolved through time to become what it is today. There are pieces of it in many of today's modern religions and cultures. In Nepal, it is a way of life, not a religion.

The more I read, the more I see that humans have manipulated these beautiful scriptures and rituals and misinterpreted them so much we are a long way from the original seeds of Hinduism or Vedic traditions. Each area of India and Nepal has its own interpretation or understanding, which is what makes it so fascinating. In part, there is freedom in how you choose to honour this faith. Of course, there are those who have manipulated the faith for power and their own gain, but if you can get beneath that, you can see the underlying messages.

My interpretation so far is that, like Buddhism, it is an invitation to connect and live in harmony with others and the planet. It is about being conscious, it is about creation, and it is about balance. Above all, the feminine and masculine roles are beautifully articulated through metaphor and stories, yet often misinterpreted, they have meaning. It is about unity. It is about merging both shadow and light and moving towards Samadhi (peace and enlightenment). I've been following an American, David Frawley, an amazing scholar on Hinduism, and his interpretations and understanding of this ancient tradition are amazing. I think so much of it has been lost. He is trying to resurrect and teach people the real Hinduism; it is quite interesting listening to his interviews.

It offers so many tools to people through stories and metaphors, that if experienced in a symbolic way, can give people guidance and knowledge on how to meet, accept and rise above the challenges that life can bring. I think we need this in our lives, now more than ever, especially with the rise in mental health issues. In part, I think this is why our modern society is so sick. Russell Brand talks about this in his latest book. In an interview I watched, he expressed very clearly how being connected to something is the only way to beat addiction. He went on to suggest, and I'm inclined to agree, that addiction is rife in our world due to the lack of connection and the disconnectedness that seems to have become part of being in a modern society. We need connection to spirit, to have faith in something greater than ourselves, to have something beyond, to move towards, to keep us aligned with our heart and soul and connected to the world around us, with meaning and purpose.

I read on Facebook one time that there were some Muslim women saying that they liked their burkas and other aspects of being female and Muslim, and many people struggled to understand this. Many people judged them. Something I have observed here is that women in Nepal are extremely capable and strong and although there are many areas in which the women could develop, I can appreciate certain aspects of the role of women here. For me, I have never felt more feminine and in touch with my goddess self than in Nepal.

In Nepal I could settle more into the feminine energy and did not need to be the tough woman. Maybe it is because for a long time in Nepali culture, the roles were so clearly defined. Women have very important roles, as do the men. There is no confusion around the roles. It is mostly just an automatic place in which they arrive. Some people may view this as oppressive. I disagree, not in all cases. In many cases the women would not have it any other way, they want to be the matriarch of the family and take pride in this role. They understand the importance of their role in the community and are revered for it when they do it well.

The men are equally proud of their role to protect and provide for the family. Of course, in more recent times in the city areas, this is changing with the external influence of the internet. However, this is clearly coming from projections from the developed countries that being a 'mother' is not a career in itself and that women should strive for more. Hence, so many women in developed countries are wearing so many hats, trying to maintain and balance their careers and raise children, hence mother guilt exists. Would mother guilt exist in Nepal? Don't misunderstand me here, I am not talking about the extreme issues against women such as trafficking and limiting beliefs surrounding their capabilities. I am merely highlighting sometimes as outsiders we are quick to judge that their lives are meaningless without education or a career, or that serving their husbands is not fair. We often miss the point, as we are only looking through our modern women's lens.

Women do serve their husbands here and are proud to do so, and where this is unfair is, when it is exploited, goes unappreciated or is disrespected. A fair and just marriage in Nepal would see that the man is equally of service to the woman, however his role in doing this is very different. Witnessing this for me in action has been life-changing around my idea of marriage and relationship.

In Nepal, public displays of affection are not allowed between men and women. At first, I thought this was small-minded, and they needed to change that. I was confused by it, I felt that this was adding to the oppression of people and their frustrations, potentially being expressed as aggression.

After being in Nepal, living in the communities for a while, I started seeing the gold in this boundary. I realised that by keeping some things special and sacred, it built more intimacy between people. It alleviated so many unnecessary emotions that often surround relationships. There were clear boundaries, and when we were together, I felt I had his complete focus and attention. I felt as though this energy was saved for me and then given to me in the privacy of our home. It created an intensity of love and understanding I felt privileged to share with only him.

It created trust and a feeling that we shared something secret that no one else knew about. I started to look forward to the alone time with Govin, so that we could express our feelings and affection. It actually brought us closer together. I found we did not take for granted the love we had for each other. I experienced reverence and respect, new feelings I had never experienced before, yet somehow remembered. I found we had more passion this way; it opened up more communication, and we expressed our feelings more readily. It is so funny how quick we can be to judge things from our limited view, without immersion into the experience. Experience changes everything, especially judgment and view.

There is gold in keeping clear boundaries in relationships. There is gold in knowing what roles we are to play. It provides a level of certainty, safety and security. People know what to do. It can be helpful in communities in order to get the work done, just as it is in a business, we do the role we were assigned to do. It does not mean we cannot change our roles. However, it is important to know what the roles are and what role we are playing or want to play. What happens in the home between two people is sacred and not for public scrutiny, opinion or view. In my view, keeping some personal space and mystery in the relationship can actually be very healthy. I believe it allows you space to move towards each other willingly. For me, it meant I could consciously connect in the present moment and express my love fully in the sacred space we created, without fear of judgement. I enjoyed the privacy, the sacredness of our space. Love can be experienced, displayed, and given to us in a myriad of ways. We just need to be open enough to receive it and not judge it.

Honestly, I see love in everything. Love exists everywhere, if you look deep enough and past your own fears of what is not there.

So many of us live with an expectation or a view of what things should look like, feel like, be like, and this is the biggest killer of dreams and relationships. Expectation is the biggest creator of disappointment. Every time I had expectations in my life and not had them met, I'd experienced feelings of rejection, unworthiness, uncertainty or feeling alone in the world. It created suffering in me that always threw me into a pit of depression. On the biggest losses, I would grieve so hard with my heart broken that I would even consider ending my life. I now truly believe that it is safer and a better way to be in the world if I have no expectations. I have felt the loss and grief of unmet expectations, and it is too much to bear. I now look to acceptance and choose to not expect as much as I can, and try my best to work with what is there, what is present. I set intentions and goals, however I always make sure they are aligned with my heart and values and I do my best to communicate these to others so that we are clear. I love that in my relationships now; I am learning to communicate more effectively so that everybody is clear. I've changed the energy of expectation to one of communication and acceptance of the things that I control or change. Now I communicate openly without fear of what I need or want in a relationship with the other person. A person with high expectations has an ego that believes that it is in control of the world and others. The universe will send an equal amount of chaos to match or balance out the control you perceive that you have.

In Ayurvedic medicine, we are reminded that we are in a relationship with everything, constant communion, whether or not we are aware of it. When

I opened my heart to acceptance and allowed myself to receive without condition, I got to see the blessings and the gold. I am enjoying exploring relationships in this way and I am enjoying seeing the blessings.

In the majority of Nepali communities, women wear 'kurta', 'sari' or 'lungi'. In the beginning, I enjoyed the beautiful bright colours all swirling and moving. Everywhere we went in Nepal there was this beautiful rainbow of movement. But then, through my western lens, I'd started to question whether they were being made to wear these things. As with our perception of the 'burka', I wondered whether this was expected by the men in the community and another way of suppressing the women. I chatted with some women, both modern ones in the cities, who were wearing western fashion, and the village women. It was interesting to note that they both had very different views, so I decided to wear the kurta and sari myself and see what happened. In dressing this way, I first noted that I felt beautiful in a goddessy kind of way. The colours made me feel alive and the flowing cotton fabrics made me feel light and free in my body, almost like the feeling of wearing pyjamas. I did not feel like an object of desire, yet I still felt beautiful, but I felt that we all looked beautiful in our kurtas. The fashion and comparititus disappeared for me.

I remember dressing up one day in the sari with all the bangles, earrings and fanciness of a princess for the local Teej festival. It struck me that perhaps the locals felt differently to me, in that they compared saris and still experienced the pressure felt by many women in the world to look beautiful. Despite this, I still felt that the 'sexiness' element that exists in our western world was less of a desire amongst these women. For them, it was more about looking beautiful like a princess and being desired as potential marriage material, a goddess. I concluded I could never truly understand another culture without living in it and learning about it through immersion. Experience is truly the only way to understand and learn in this world.

Chapter 16
There Are Sometimes No Words

It is a funny thing being in a place for an extended period where English is not the first language. I realised how much I relied on the input of others in my life, for confirmation, for validation, and interaction in many forms. It had really made me see how much I seek outside of myself, for re-assurance and comfort. It was these musings I often contemplated during this monsoon time. I could not have these conversations here and get feedback or reassurance, as English was the second language for many. Even if they could understand, their understanding of my world was minimal. My habit of always needing to share my thoughts with others became apparent to me. One reason I might have felt so frustrated for so much of my life and spent a lot of time procrastinating was because I'd allow too much energy in from outsiders. I allowed others' opinions and views to sway my own. I was now beginning to experience that deep knowing that the answers and clarity always come from within.

Despite many Nepali people learning English at school, and quite well I will add, it was the thinking processes that were quite different. Considering the differences between Sanskrit languages and Latin, I was impressed with the level at which they had learnt English. The more I tried to learn their language and culture, the more of an outsider I felt; the more alone I felt, the more I realised the depth of the Nepali culture and its people. Just learning a language was not quite enough to really understand another culture. It was around this time that I started to write and express my thoughts; I started needing that space away from people to get my thoughts out. I was not expressing them like I usually would over coffee with friends or at my work. Instead, I found writing created space in my mind, from the accumulation of thoughts and energy not being expressed.

I became more aware of my tendencies to use people around me to distract me from my heart's desire. I learnt that I always took care of and listened to everyone else first. I was great at fixing everyone else's problems first; I was always last. I saw my pattern clearly for the first time, as I could not be distracted quite so easily here. My thoughts were with me. A new feeling and experience for me, as life here was slow, it was almost like I became aware of the thoughts flowing through me for the first time, like in a meditation. It was an opportunity to spend time with me. I was in communication with all parts of myself and beyond myself.

I saw moments in life where I'd experienced not getting my expectations met. Sacrificing my values for the comfort of knowing I was liked and the moments where I would get fed up with giving away my power all the time and cut out everything. Like a child throwing a tantrum, not getting what it wants and then throwing its toys from the pram. Although at the time it often felt good to cleanse, it was also often a desperate cry from my inner child to be heard. The moments of self-sabotage that often took months to recover from, the self-loathing and judgment of yet another failed goal. My perception had been that if I did not complete something that it was a failure.

At the same time I was seeing the shadow, I also realised the perfection of the past, for all it had been teaching me; about my patterns, my people pleasing tendencies and willingness to run myself ragged before spitting the dummy and retreating from the world, tail between my legs. To all the people that thought I was running away from my problems in wanting to travel and be in Nepal, I would argue it brought me closer to me. I was now seeing more clearly than ever. So much of our modern society is designed to keep us so distracted that people are disconnected from self, others, the food they eat, everything they do and the land they inhabit.

Ask yourself when you book a holiday every year if it is to escape? And when you do, do you fill that space up too? With so much action you still fail to connect with you, others and the planet, only to return and feel longing to get back there and not feeling rested at all? Solitude, space, and beingness can be healing.

Chapter 17
Kali Doesn't Allow Maps

Just when you think you know where you are going, Kali will flip it; always bringing you back in line with your heart, your dharma, your truth, if you allow yourself to feel her power and screams. She is the one who will always rip your head off your shoulders, bringing you crashing back down into your heart. The heart journey is not for the fainthearted. It is a journey of courage and vulnerability. You cannot have one without the other. It does not care about the material things of this world.

It was around this time of self-reflection during the monsoon that I made one of the hardest decisions. The earthquake and all that followed was a massive deconstruction of belief systems, of my values, of so much of what I was. It was like getting a download or an upgrade of the mainframe. People Helping People had been operating in Nepal delivering aid for about five months at this stage and I was seeing things around the project that were not aligned with my heart. In hindsight, it was created with the remnants of my old belief systems and constructs and as the downloads were coming to completion; I was quickly realising that this was not my path. Like the decision to send my daughter with her father after months of custody battles and thousands of dollars; I realised I had to face the very thing I was resisting. People Helping People International (PHPI) was the group that was formed from the guest house immediately after the earthquake.

Early on, I had made it clear to the group my intention and goals around helping people, empowering people, and connecting with people. Responding from the needs of the people, not from a place of projection or western standards, but from a place of validation and recognition of the needs and values of the recipients, without our projections.

Connection with the locals was paramount, in my view, to helping them. I was so passionate about this creation. It was rolling along beautifully, with people co-ordinating, coming together over a common goal to help those in need after the earthquake. That made the following decision so hard. For the past five months, I had watched this group come together on my belief and faith that we could make a difference. I was humbled and in awe, and in part I don't think I could believe that we were doing it, having an impact. I had somehow brought the Nepali crew and foreigner crew together to make a difference to the victims of the earthquake. Even now it feels like a distant dream I had. We had gathered every night at 6 p.m. to discuss what we could commit to the next day.

In the beginning, it worked beautifully. Everyone had a special role based on their specific and unique skills. The energy and momentum that came after the first mission was amazing. After a little while, I noticed the foreigners did not work with the Nepali people well at all, always coming from a place of 'I know better'. Often reacting or wanting to do something based on their own emotional needs or from their view of how things should go rather than validating and working with the local people. I found this challenging to observe and manage. I could not understand why they could not see the value of working with the locals. It was their country, their terrain, their communities and I felt who better to understand the needs of the Nepali people than the people themselves? Not to mention the healing available to them in being able to support their neighbours at such a trying time. This frustrated me a lot as I was becoming the meat in the sandwich. Equally, the Nepali crew were also coming to me to complain about the 'stupid' tourists not knowing anything and spending too much money. Unfortunately, neither party could recognise they needed each other. Doing my best, I stayed in the co-ordinating role and kept things running as best as possible, focusing on people management. Which I guess was my strength, however, I really wanted to dedicate more of my time to the locals and supporting them.

We got out to thirteen villages and at least $25,000 AUD of the funds came from my crowdfunding site alone.

I was so humbled by the trust and faith so many of my family and friends had in me and the way they donated so generously was so inspiring and motivating.

For the first time in my life, I experienced the feeling of being on purpose, truly aligned with my heart, connected and contributing to something greater than myself. I felt like I had found my 'calling'. After three months of our little operation, the talks started gathering momentum around creating an NGO. At first, I was hesitant because I felt why change what is working? Then, as we chatted more, I saw the bigger picture and thought, well, yes, I wanted to ultimately make this a part of my life; empowering, assisting, and inspiring people through active change. I knew the issues and ongoing support that was needed in Nepal was a long-term thing that went beyond the earthquake disaster. I got on board, but with some reservations floating about my head around integrity and authenticity, and questioned if we were on the same page.

After some weeks, it was clear the other members of our small crew were coming from a different angle to what I thought we'd agreed upon. The more I tried to voice my concerns about it, the more I felt disconnected from the group. I felt disempowered and isolated. The Americans seemed to have so much more ego and determination about doing things their way. Every time I suggested anything, it felt like it was rejected before I'd even got it all out.

I wanted to work on projects that would teach a man to fish, so to speak. If I am honest here, my self-doubt started to rise. We were considering earth bag buildings. I felt that if we could get the Nepali people to these courses, then they could go out easily and help other Nepali people to rebuild. Then there were the relief missions that kept coming in and the team wanted to save the money to create the NGO and not help the missions anymore. This did not sit well with me, as I felt that the money was donated with the intent to go directly to villages and relief and that was what I'd been promoting from day dot. Slowly my ego and self-doubt started getting in the way and slowly I retreated and disconnected further. I was questioning if perhaps I was wrong, as we had all agreed that no money could be spent unless we all agreed on the mission. I felt I had no voice, no purpose, feeling like a failure and second guessing myself.

The next few weeks were a tumultuous to-ing and fro-ing of emotions and conflict between my heart and head. All the while being aware of the energies and needs of the Nepali people and the whole reason I'd stayed there post-earthquake.

After the earthquake, I'd felt so clear about helping people. The energies that came flooding in April to support my vision were overwhelming and amazing. I'd felt so clear and present, and now I was filled with doubt. To be honest, I think that somewhere along the way the energy went to my head. My head took over from my heart and I'd got caught up in the people management, lost connection with my values and with the people. The idea of creating an NGO and a structured organisation to continue with Aid became my focus and appealed to my ego's need for status and significance. This took me away from the needs right here and now. All the while, this small voice was saying, What are you doing? Are you sure this is what is required? I'd stopped listening to the guidance and had been swept up in the magnitude of it all.

Sometimes when we get clarity, the mind gets so excited that it shifts into doing and knowing; it takes control again, and it thinks it knows exactly what is needed.

As soon as this happens, we are being led by our ego again. Living from the heart requires surrender. It requires not knowing; it requires allowing yourself to be guided gently without urgency and the need to conquer and achieve. But to be present each day, taking action and responding to the call of the energies that present themselves at that given moment. This is how I teach every class. It never fails. As soon as I think I know what to expect, or what, or how to teach, I have failed or am disappointed.

How can I be present in the hearts of the class if I'm not completely open and receptive? The teacher is also the student.

Everything I'd left behind in Australia was structured and bound in policies and procedures and governance. To be part of creating that here in Nepal in a country that already has so many NGOs and do-gooders, I just couldn't stomach it. Because that was precisely why we had been so busy in the first place. Whilst all the NGOs and government groups were meeting on 'how' to help the Nepali people (spend their money), we had been responding to the people. I felt that so much of that world had already failed the Nepali people. They just needed people to respond and take action without all the channels of hierarchy and process. In Nepal seemed to take twice as long as in the western world. These people needed food, shelter and, most of all, they needed to be heard. The other issues would be taken care of in the future, but for now, that's all we needed to do.

Literally purging after carrying around this feeling of doubt and conflict for a couple of months, I spent twenty-four hours in bed with gastro. My heart was aware I was veering off the path I'd so vulnerably embarked upon just four months before. I am not saying that NGOs didn't have an important place in Nepal. They did and do amazing work. I was sharing what was coming up for me and what was aligned with my heart. I am much more organic and creative, and I realized I had a different direction to go in. I knew deep down this was just the beginning. Nepal and I had only just begun a lifelong connection.

For some people, I am sure I am nothing but frustration; I know for my ex-husband this was definitely the case. Even my parents find my way of going through life uncertain and scary for them. I am sure they have wanted to tear their hair out with how I choose to live from this flowing organic heart space. However, for me it is the best way to keep harmony and peace within myself. Living this way has brought me to this amazing place in my life, that just keeps getting more expansive. I would not trade my experiences and life for anything. I value experience over matter any day. If I follow other people's ideals and expectations, I will always end up burnt out and depressed, and ultimately, my soul will die. I had learnt this much in my life so far.

Kali had other plans for me. As soon as I thought I knew where I was going, she ripped my head off again, leaving me with nowhere else to go but back to my heart. It always happens the same way; when I am sick of the conflict between my heart and head, I ask for some guidance and there she is, instantly, swiftly slicing my head off; so the path is clear, the blood flows again from my heart and the path is cleared of debris.

Energy goes where energy flows. Well, this is what it feels like for me when I'm stuck on my path, with the ego wanting to take charge. It was always quite a painful experience and was certainly related to my awareness level of the situation. The more I resisted the opportunity to connect to my heart, the more I suffered between the head and the heart. Finding myself procrastinating and frustrated at not being able to see or control the situation. I now welcome Kali when I find myself in this pattern.

When creativity is stifled, I am stifled and sink quickly into overwhelm and the abyss of powerlessness. The only way I have found to maintain energy flow is to embrace change and to trust where my heart leads. To flow like water, like the river Kali Gandaki, constantly flowing and cleansing away the debris. Sometimes scary and destructive, but always creating a new pathway through the mountains.

I continued mentoring and supporting other Nepali crews who were doing some great work with local Nepali donations. I was impressed with their enthusiasm and work. Without the dollars behind me, we worked together and gathered another $10,000 through fundraising efforts locally. We put on an event at the local club where some famous Nepali musicians came and entertained the crowd for approximately $20 a ticket. This was expensive in Nepali terms, yet the turnout was amazing, and lots of people and businesses donated to make this a successful event. It felt great to work alongside these locals in this way, watching them empower themselves without the help of outside aid.

Soon it was clear to me, I needed to reconnect to myself and work out what I needed to do for me. The above experience helped me to see how quickly outsiders can judge undeveloped countries and make big assumptions that they know better, and I did not want to be a part of that energy. I released the need to be part of the People Helping People crew and resigned for them to go on without me.

It was honestly a weird feeling. I did not realise how attached I'd become to this creation. I dreamt it into being literally two nights after the earthquake. From co-creating with others, to become disconnected and letting it go after all that we had experienced and achieved. Even though I initially felt ashamed to let go, almost like giving up (past programming), I realised later that it was right; I had to trust and have faith that this was not my path. I tried my best to distract myself, and the more I did that, the more I felt disempowered and disconnected.

'A genuine seeker, a person who develops an urge within, will always find his/ her guru. He/she may find it in a man, in a woman, or he/she may find it in a rock. He/she will definitely find it somewhere, there is no doubt about it.'

SADGHURU

Chapter 18
Who's Your Guru?

A friend once said to me, 'It is your expectation that has caused your suffering and or disappointment'.

I believe that most people experience life this way, whether or not they are aware. The monk Thich Nhat Hanh talked a lot about this in his life. That the space between where we are and where someone else is expected to be is the space where we suffer. I'm inclined to agree with him, and I also believe you can find your guru anywhere. The reason is that the guru is within you. When you experience resonance through a guru's teachings, you are realising yourself. Your highest self.

I have been exploring this for a while now and in my life have read many books from OSHO to Kahil Gibran to Wayne Dyer. I have listened to podcasts and most agree the importance of dropping expectation will undoubtedly minimise our suffering. Eckhart Tolle's book, 'The power of NOW', is probably the one that focuses fully on the concept of acceptance and being in the now.

Through a variety of experiences I realised that sometimes to make connection we have to disconnect, or at least experience the shadow side, being disconnected. It is fundamentally how we humans evolve and learn. Once we understand the shadow, it seems we can move forward. What if we turned to the shadow instead? Chose to dive into it and see what is there? What if we saw the shadow as our curriculum/philosophy/belief through which our guru is teaching us? Would we then be more willing to receive the wisdom that is there?

We are connecting and disconnecting all the time in micro and macro ways. Slowly, through writing, I was brought back to me, to my heart, and I slowly realised the amazing lesson I had just received. I had become too attached to the outcome, to control everything around me, and I had been more concerned with being liked. I'd lost my purpose along the way and had started becoming like the people I was not wanting to be. I was holding on too tightly to PHPI, suffocating it, not allowing others in to assist and grow.
\
The very thing I was trying to create, collective contribution to community, had become the Kate show. I had become quite possessive and created a picture and expectation of how things should be. I had to be honest, my ego had been bruised. The operation started not needing me and started taking on its own energy, becoming a different entity. My ego felt obsolete. I was not certain about my vision or my role. I had given away my personal power and forgot to establish who I was within this creation. So others' values and energies were able to transform it into what they were visioning. I'd allowed others with a stronger sense of self and what they wanted to create to overshadow my vision, and instead of stepping up, I stepped out. I self-sabotaged it because I stopped believing in my dream and ultimately stopped believing in myself. I'd doubted.

'When you stay on purpose and refuse to be discouraged by fear, you align with the infinite self, in which all possibilities exist.,' Wayne Dyer said.

In my need to control, I crushed all the possibilities of how I could be a part of an evolving process.

I took a walk to Fewa Lake and enjoyed the beautiful serenity. I enjoyed breakfast and focused on the bigger vision and chatted to a volunteer about projects. This was quite useful in moving me out of victim space and recognising that I'm here to contribute to something far greater than trivial things. To once again let go, learn the lesson, integrate it and move on. I felt a bit better after that and started working on forgiving myself for the mistakes I'd made with PHPI.

I headed back to my flat and after a cool shower and some yoga stretches, I moved into the child's pose, a soothing and nurturing pose. I felt the emotion well up. It was like the physical body moved into a child's pose with no prompting from thought and it just instantly opened up my hurt inner child and I started to cry. The little girl who felt powerless to change anything was once again awoken and reminded of the past. A little girl who was often told that the world could not be changed, that it was not her problem; that there were powerful things out there and that she did not have the skills or tools to deal with them.

I stayed there for at least five minutes, just allowing every bit of emotion to flow out of my eyes and body. It felt quite surreal, like it was not even me. I allowed it anyway and decided to love myself a little more.

I sat naked with my sarong around me, in the corner of my room with the fan on. It was so hot and humid that day, in fact like every day during the monsoon, and thought for a moment, now, would be a great time to do a heart chakra meditation. I found one of my favourite tracks online, sat quietly and just let the words and sounds slowly transport me, transform me and allow me to receive. WOW! Forgiveness, Love, Acceptance. Next, I asked gently in my mind if there was anything I needed to know: a soft gentle, patient voice, a voice so familiar and ancient, the ever-present one that travels lifetimes, simply said, Let it go.

Then, when you feel constriction, when you feel that you're closing or withdrawing, that is the time to open more, give more, be more. It is where the growth happens... it is the end of a cycle and rebirth of a new one. It is done.

Transformation can only happen after we move into acceptance and allow the energy to move through us.

The next day, things shifted again; I came out of my slump. I started writing a proposal for a rebuilding project, emailing key people who could assist us with the project, wrote more of my blog, and booked a short holiday. Communication and connection had returned. Suddenly I was feeling more me again, refocused, realigned, and motivated to move forward. Things had changed.

Sometimes the most challenging environments ask you to go deeper to find the strength within yourself. It felt like I had found a map to move me out of my ego and self-sabotaging tendencies. I'd become aware of expansion and contraction, allowing, flowing, and letting go. I'd consciously done it this time. For the first time in my life, I had consciously turned and faced it and chosen to let go. This was a different feeling versus the forced letting go that was often the case in my past. Disconnection had become a conscious reconnection. I had learned to create, contribute, then destruct, disconnect, become conscious, reconnect, create, contribute, then destruct. It was a never-ending cycle of growth. One that is happening whether we are conscious or not. However, in being conscious and choosing it, it flowed so much better. This was what it felt like to experience conscious living.

This experience taught me to become aware of disconnection, to stop and allow the feelings to enter and ask them what needed to change. So now I know when I'm entering some sort of change cycle, that it is okay just to accept and move through it. To face it. We are transitioning and it is only ever temporary.

Nepal is a land of contradictions and contrasts. It is a place that could consume you and at the same time open your heart in massive proportions. After five months, it still fascinated me; the people, the culture, the way of being, the cows wandering the streets (I think this will always make me giggle, no matter how many times I witness it). The way people had no personal space and no matter where you went, there were people watching you (this I still find challenging). The idea that public affection is kept behind closed doors, for someone like me, a tricky one. Yet it was always embracing me and teaching me.

It was like there was harmony and peace within the chaos and hardship. It was a lesson I needed to learn. I often had trouble accepting things I could not change. A contrast of ideas so far removed from my world in

Australia, yet for some reason, I felt like it had provided me with the balance and challenges I needed. In Nepal, nothing is hidden.

It gave me courage to take action in my life and follow my heart, to not be afraid and to embrace uncertainty and ultimately recognise my dharma.

Chapter 19
False Evidence Appearing Real

In my view, our modern world is lacking faith. We are all so used to certainty and controlled environments we need this in all areas of our lives. So much so that people have denounced spirit, religion and many things that are connected with the mysteries of life. I really believe that mental health conditions such as depression and anxiety are on the rise in modern society as the result of a sick society that has no faith in anything, with one-dimensional attitudes that just disregard the mysteries and uncertainty of life. Science is wonderful and has made some wonderful contributions to our world, however I do not believe that it can ever be the absolute. It is not possible to find the answers to everything in a Petri dish or mathematical equation. Even if we could, it does not change the fact that we can never know everything. Some things are just because. Actually, to think all the answers are in science can be a very masculine way of viewing the world. To me, the only absolute in this world is change.

Every time we try to control our environment, we are setting ourselves up for mental disturbance and frustration. It is not possible for us to control anything other than how we respond to the constant changes and fluctuations that exist all around us every day. Faith is an important component for dealing with this uncertainty.

A person without faith in something is a person disconnected. To me, they are almost robotic, and they never question anything.

They just accept that things are the 'norm' and go about their daily lives trying to keep everything the same.

If we live completely in the mind, we will always be looking for logic, reason and control, and this keeps us disconnected from the universe and everything in it. The mind is brilliant as a servant to the heart, however, the mind as the only source of knowing is devoid of any wonder, magic, creativity or love. Basically disconnected from life itself.

Some people talk about hope; for example, 'I hope things change', or 'I do hope he changes'. I think hope is disempowering and faith plays a different role than hope. Let's explore this a bit more.

Faith is the unwavering, knowing that you are held by a force greater than yourself. It is a knowing that even though you do not understand what is happening around you, you know it is temporary and has a purpose, even if you do not know in the moment. It is more active than hope. Hope puts faith in being rescued, whereas faith understands that every action has a higher purpose and, therefore, we can never be denied. It is a connection to something deeper, a deep-rooted knowingness that requires no answers.

It stops searching. It is a different kind of acceptance. Faith can only be experienced in the heart; it is connected to courage and vulnerability. In fact, the only way to turn FEAR into courage is to have 'faith'. If you are someone who lives in the mind, faith will seem futile and silly, not useful at all. You might think it is naïve, however, I would argue that until you have experienced it and felt the feeling of being helped and guided, then you would not know what faith is. Faith requires a devotion and a love for all of experience, for the blessing of life.

It is without judgment. It allows everything and suppresses nothing. It is gratitude disguised, because in that moment, although all might seem overwhelmingly challenging, you know it is a necessary contraction that will ultimately lead you to expansion. When we have faith in something, gratitude, joy and grace will always follow.

Throughout history, humans have been led to have faith in gods, goddesses, religions, mythical creatures, fairy folk, rituals and the sacred. This faith has been invoked and used in some of the most challenging times in human history. Faith has been used in the moments of 'I do not "know" what else to do'. It is in that moment that faith drops you in to the heart, courage is found, and we finally surrender to the journey, to our dharma and karma. This is important to understand, because so often we think the answer to everything lies in the mind, in the brain. This type of knowing is different, it is not expansive, it is not creative, it cannot evolve as you do.

True knowing comes from the heart and to find it, you must have faith, because it takes courage to follow your heart. It can defy science, logic, norms and many things that keep us stuck. We are perfectly designed this way, yet so many of us have forgotten and have become disconnected from this way of being in alignment in these modern times. To have faith meant believing that something more intelligent and bigger than yourself was at work; the mysterious, this takes us out of the ego. However, the irony is that at some time in history, some humans decided we were not worthy of knowing about the mysterious through our own connection and decided we needed to follow a human or authority who knew better. So slowly, we became accustomed to accessing the spiritual part of ourselves through a third party, such as a priest, a king, a shaman, a church, a temple, and so on. We created hierarchy. Over time, this moved us towards a disconnection from self, spirit, and the universe. It separated us and unfortunately for many of us, slowly we forgot we are a part of the same source of creation as the gods we were worshipping.

We are divinity; when we are connected, we are guided, we are supported and held. Faith in this keeps us connected, knowing that everything is in perfect balance and has a purpose, even if we cannot comprehend it at this time. It is about the realisation that we are all in this together and that is where the power is. Conscious, connected, collective communities all contributing to something greater than ourselves. Working directly with the source, being divinely guided through our dharma. We are all born with a blueprint to our own souls. Faith keeps the ego in check. We need the ego, we need the mind, but we need to use it to support our dharma, our soul's journey, not to drive the bus. It is an advisor of sorts, but not the king. In the past, having faith in your king, queen, your leader or religion meant giving your power away to something greater than yourself. At the time, people accepted that and possibly enjoyed being able to give that responsibility to another source greater than themselves. I believe that these power-hungry authorities enjoyed being given this power as much as the people were happy to give away their responsibility. In many ways, we are still doing this today. It is much easier to blame the government, your boss, your partner, or parents than to take responsibility for your own path, right?

Today we have evolved to understand that we create every moment that exists through our intent and actions, so too does the universe. We are co-creating with the universe, with each other, with the planet. Everything is connected. Everything is in absolute relationship with everything else. We are fragments, pieces of creation, all creating and being created. So, we have a responsibility to each other and ourselves, to stay connected and to have faith in the universal intelligence that is creating with us, and allow it the space to respond to us and manifest within us and through us.

Chapter 20
Shiva and Shakti

The 1st of Saaun, (16 July to the 16 August) was the start of the month-long Hindu tradition of Shrawan Sankratin, where women worshipped the God Shiva and also their husbands or future husbands. The Nepalese women seemed to embrace and enjoy this time. They looked forward to celebrating the goddess within and devoting their prayers and offerings to the God Shiva and fasting for their husband's longevity.

Part of this celebration meant they would dress in their best saris and kurtas. If they were already married, it was usually green or red, as these are the colours of married women. The younger women would wear other colours and many would paint henna/mahendi designs on their hands as a sign that they were praying for a husband or loved one. They would wear red, green, and yellow bracelets, six or twelve at a time. They looked so pretty with all these colours and bracelets up their arms, always jingling as they moved. I later learned that the henna designs would always have secret initials hidden in the design to represent the boyfriend, lover, or husband. So it was quite fun looking at the hands trying to find the initials of their loved one; lots of embarrassed giggles and teasing were going on in parlours everywhere.

For some women in developed countries, this might seem a little chauvinistic or one sided to worship men in this way. However, as much as Nepal is a patriarchal society, this was another opportunity for me to see the power of the goddess and women in Nepal. At first, when this tradition was explained to me, I was thinking, 'how one sided and oppressive'. It was easy to think like that as an Australian from a country where women are often doing roles the same as men – especially in my case as a single mother I had become accustomed to relying on no man. The more I observed and experienced the women in Nepal, the more I could appreciate another view. I made a mental note to try to not look through Australian eyes and immerse myself in the experience.

I asked Govin to tell me more about this tradition and of course I googled away and learnt as much as I could in a short time. The next day, I was guided to the Shiva temple, all dressed up in my green and blue sari. At this stage, I was not married, so the ladies told me I was praying for my secret lover. They did not know it was Govin, although I am sure they guessed.

They guided me through the process. I needed to pray and worship Shiva with an offering of fruit, rice, coconut and milk, then I had to ask Shiva to bless Govin. I went through the process and something about it felt natural. It was an intentional prayer and a moment that I was completely devoted to praying for another person, afterwards they told me I had to pray to Shiva and fast every Monday for the month of Saaun, Shrawan.

This was also recognised as good health practice to ward off nasty monsoonal illnesses, so I set the intention and adhered to the practice. I meditated every Monday morning to the beautiful mantras of 'Sacred Earth's Om Namah Shivaya' and listening to Prem's beautiful voice as I imagined Shiva sitting in front of me. I found the process of worshipping the masculine energy of Shiva quite soothing. It was like the more I acknowledged the masculine, the more feminine I became. I liked it. I felt softer, more open, and less like I had to hold it all together and be strong. It was interesting to note that Shiva is known as the 'the destroyer' and or the 'transformer'. Govin thought I was funny

participating, then later he told me he really liked that I was learning about his culture, and I was enjoying it too.

My intention had been to learn more about the Nepalese women and the deeper meanings of the Hindu traditions and way of life. I witnessed Hindu rituals and offerings woven into their everyday lives. It was just a way of being in Nepal, such as blessing their husbands by putting their heads to their husband's feet. Alternately, the sons also put their heads to their mother's feet. I noticed the regular offerings to altars and temples and Govin's mother would often tell us we could not travel at 12 p.m. It was an auspicious time to travel, she said. It was an odd request, but I honoured it anyway. Govin said he never challenged his mother's views about keeping the ancestors happy. Whenever we would leave the house on a journey, we were blessed with a tikka on our foreheads by both his parents. Actually, the offering of blessings in the form of tikkas was a part of everyday life here. Tikkas are a part of Hindu culture and are created with rice and coloured with red dye. They are used in prayer, ritual and between people throughout as blessings. To understand the full meaning of tikka is too long to go into here, however I can roughly translate it to represent us being the conduits to Shiva and how the god energy drives the human experience on this planet. There are other simpler meanings, however, for me, I look at the deeper aspects of the ritual and why it might have been created.

In Nepal, as a woman, I truly felt protected, almost revered, like I was special had a special divinity. It was like in Nepal I am the goddess, the goddess is me, and so the gods (men) protect her fiercely. I understand there are also a lot of cultural situations that, in Nepal and countries like this, are equally oppressive of women. However, I would argue that the pressure is on both sides of the coin. As much as women are oppressed compared to developed countries, that the men are under a lot of pressure also, in other ways. If you look from a distance, they are a product of their society, as are we of ours. I'm choosing to see the blessings in their society and, in turn, it helps me see the blessings in ours. I am aware of the atrocities that happen against women in many places around the world and I would argue that in these cases it is the distortion in their understanding, potentially where ego is running the show and it is the opposite of union. The god/ goddess, feminine and masculine, are out of balance and that is what creates these atrocities.

It is taking advantage of the vulnerability, instead of celebrating it. It is sad that this still happens, but it is important that we do not say it is because we are women, or that it is all people of these cultures. It is sadly due to the disconnectedness of these people to divinity and the ego's interpretation of their society, culture, and religion.

The level of respect I received in this country as a woman goes beyond anything I have ever experienced. I am not saying all Nepalese people are like this, however I felt we could explore this further as a society, the idea of what real respect looks and feels like. Although it is difficult sometimes to let go of western ideals, I feel it is time to explore other cultures with the view to learning how to be better humans and ultimately being better communities. Sharing wisdom and integrating knowledge, as we all have gifts to share.

I was intrigued by the apparent strength and acceptance of the women here. Even though it was difficult as a foreigner to become part of the woman's world here, as they were quite shy with foreigners and they didn't trust their English skills, over time I created some connections with Nepali women. I felt like I belonged to a sacred sisterhood that I had never felt here in Australia. Each time thereafter, when I visited Baglung, I noticed it was different. The women had become bolder and each of them was desperate to connect and learn from me. I think they had accepted me, because I had participated in their rituals openly without question. They felt respected and valued, because I had respected and valued their traditions.

As soon as Govin would leave the house to visit his friends, about six or seven women would walk and gather, squatting around the front steps of his small home. Often knitting or multi-tasking, they would ask me in broken English and simple Nepali language all kinds of questions about Australia and life as a woman there. I found it intriguing that they had no boundaries around the type of questions, especially around my relationship with their neighbour. I was the only white woman who had spent a lot of time in this village, needless to say they wanted to take advantage.

I have always believed one of the problems in Australian society is that women are becoming too masculine and that is creating a problem in our relationships with men and equally with ourselves. It is especially affecting men, as I feel many are lost and are not sure how to interact with us anymore. I feel our behaviour is creating more confused males, as in men have become a lot more cautious around women, scared to insult women or be rejected by them. I know this can be a sore subject. I am not for one minute suggesting women who have been abused in any way should not stand up and have our support. However, I have become increasingly aware of this men versus women attitude, which I believe is not the answer.

Our anger as women in the oppression or pain that has been suffered cannot be changed through retaliation, anger, blame and lashing out. We need to be careful how we handle this situation. If we use masculine energy to balance masculine energy, we will undoubtedly create more masculine energy. The way to move forward and heal this pain is to come from a connected place, a place of love, forgiveness, and femininity. Think goddess, warrior energy. I feel this is the pathway to reconnect men and women in a healthy way. We need to heal the pain through reverence, respect and validation of the roles we play. We need to work through this period of uncertainty with feminine energy; gently, lovingly, supportively and most of all patiently, allowing each other to adjust to our new understanding.

Women need to embrace the fullness of their femininity, not become more masculine, we need not fear our femininity anymore. In doing so, we will see more men embracing their feminine as well. I think so many of us fear our femininity. I think we feel that feminine equals vulnerability or weakness. This vulnerability and softness is actually our greatest strength and if we can learn about how to access this energy, then we can heal the relationship between men and women. Our fear and anger are preventing us from accessing this amazing energy. Take a moment and think of a woman giving birth. This is raw power, this is the primal feminine force in full swing. Tell me that is not powerful.

I think in our quest for equality, we have forgotten the importance of maintaining our femininity. We don't need to be the same as men. We are different; we are supposed to complement each other, not rival and compete with each other. What we need is to embrace the full power of our femininity. It is only when we can do that we will see men relax and become whole and women embrace their power and become whole. Only then will our relationships be more harmonious and productive and our roles become clear. We become partners on a quest, unioned and complementary. I believe this is what the Hindu god and goddess stories are about. The unionising of masculine and feminine as the two energies, yin and yang, night and day, sun and moon. This is what nature is always showing us. We are not seeing the strengths of being a woman; we are looking at the masculine traits and think to be strong we need to embrace more of these traits. We are focusing on the wrong parts. We still don't recognise and praise one of the most important roles that exists in the world, the mother role. Without mothers, we do not exist! It is that simple.

In modern society, we do not value the role of mother. We are always expressing through our education system, through advertising. In fact, everywhere we look, there are references that suggest being a mother is not enough, or that 'we' are not enough. How much parenting do our kids miss out on because we are trying to hold down a career, pay a mortgage, run around trying to be the perfect woman, across everything, living up to the expectations of society, that we need to have a career, perfect body and still be a perfect 1950s mum. I believe it causes the mass anxiety and depression that now exists in our societies, this feeling of constantly not being enough or not being perfect. Constantly comparing ourselves with all the other women out there.

A woman's vision is instinctually designed to take in the environment and be aware of everything that is in it. It is in our nature to care for that environment and, with the extra peripheral vision we have, this allows us to see out of the corner of our eyes and notice everything. A man's vision is designed for sharp focus and hunting. Perhaps if we start focusing and hunting like men, we will become more like them and lose our peripheral vision. Some might say this is evolution, however I disagree. I feel that one of the reasons mother nature is so sick is because we have lost our feminine side. We have lost connection with this environmental awareness. We are focusing too much on achieving and succeeding in the hunt. It saddens me a little that women have lost touch with this gift. We are designed to notice and be aware. However, this gift turned negative can become the biggest reason for our suffering. In our desire to become equal to men, we have lost touch with what it means to be a woman.

We can be women and have equal 'importance' in society and have recognition for our contributions. It does not mean we need to rival or compete with men or mimic them.

Unfortunately, so many stories of women in all cultures have been lost or misinterpreted with the intent to oppress the power of the woman. Our power has been abused in the past and that has scared the men of that time. Perhaps the men in the past feared the power of the feminine and therefore manipulated religious and spiritual texts to serve their own needs and their egos, or in their effort to 'protect' women from a place of fear. Somehow, we have all become a bit lost in our roles and responsibilities.

To me, it makes sense; Earth is known as Mother Earth. Women give birth, we create life within us. We are connected to intuition and subtle energies. We are nurturers and bring life into the world. It is time to reconnect with those parts of our-selves that are lying dormant due to society's demands. I feel when women find and reconnect with the feminine divine goddess within each of us, then we will see more balance and harmony in the world. Men come from logic and reason, and women come from emotion and feeling. All are necessary together, complementing each other and balancing each other. We are complementary. Even in LBTGQ relationships there is a feminine and masculine. It is necessary for balance. We are perfectly designed to complement each other, not rival each other or compete. Sometimes it is necessary to fight, but we need to come together, and do it together. Men and women fighting together for change, to assist, to lift up and improve the situations of our fellow humans that are still stuck in oppression.

After visiting a Nepalese wedding, and later being a bride in one, it became clearer and better understood by me the difference between the male and female roles, family values and commitments to each other. I am not saying the Hindu marriage is perfect. I am seeing a view that I find comforting and supportive. I am feeling for the first time this release; I am experiencing a feeling of safety, and for the first time in a relationship, I feel like I can breathe, be human and be supported for who I am. It feels amazing to know that I am part of an equal half that has got me if I need it and vice versa.

I am enjoying witnessing the rituals, the traditions, and reverence for life that is apparent in this ancient culture. They have festivals that honour women, that honour men, that honour animals and even machines. It is gratitude and acceptance that exists here in daily life, an understanding of the importance and necessity of all things, including the elderly. Nothing is hidden from view here. There is knowing, acceptance, and witnessing of life from all angles. I realised that this experience was healing my depression. It was allowing the shadows to surface without suppression. When you can see and experience all facets of life, then you can accept life in all its imperfections and perfections. So much of this is hidden from us in Australia. Every day in Australia the ugly, the sick, the frail, the dirty parts of being human are hidden, we are censored constantly and most of us are unaware of this.

The longer we live in this illusion, the further we will disconnect, creating depression. Depression is a symptom of our society's disconnection. The elderly are hidden in homes, there are special schools for the disabled children, there are hospitals that hide the sick, the rubbish is at the tip, and even then we are now learning that recycling is a farce. Yes, of course these modern things are what make our part of the world beautiful. Of course we need hospitals, rubbish disposals, and the like. This is also contributing to our disconnect, because the more we are not confronted by the realities of human existence the more we cannot deal with our own shadows and imperfections. We are living in an illusion of fake control and fake beauty.

Many of us when we are confronted by the ugliness of life, we cannot cope, hence depression and anxiety medication managing all the stressed-out people trying to maintain a sense of normality and control. I am not saying it does not exist in Nepal and other cultures. Of course it does. However, I've noticed that depression in these cultures is more to do with the physical body, in that they physically cannot change their situation, which results in powerlessness. I feel the depression being experienced in our part of the world, however, is directly connected to being disconnected from the realities of humanness and the planet. It seems to be a different experience or set of triggers.

Buddha's story is a perfect example of this life we are living in developed countries. He was disconnected through being royalty. When he went into the world, after years of living in luxury and hidden from all the ugliness of life, he felt compelled to explore outside the castle walls. Then he saw reality for the first time. Buddha was so taken aback by what he saw he could not go back to being the same person as he was before. Thus, he was thrust into a search for meaning and to understand suffering. I feel that in the western world we are kind of like the Buddha as a young prince; living in our palace, disconnected from reality. Except the difference being deep down, we know we are not seeing the truth and some of us secretly prefer to turn a blind eye, for fear of seeing the shadow side. I have found the shadows are where you will find the deepest love and truth.

The symbolism in Nepali culture is so deep and ancient that I am sure many Nepalese are not even sure why they do the rituals they do. They respect them deeply, though, and for most of them, it is a heartfelt experience. However, due to the caste systems, many of them have grown up ignorant of the ancient Vedic texts on which their faith was built. Therefore, they do not question their faith. The sacrifices and the ways people live and love here, it is something you can only experience.

I often felt like the Buddha here, wandering through the villages, witnessing and observing the ugliness and the beauty of life, magnificently woven together. It was during this time I learnt about love. The depth of love and the way it moves through us all. That no amount of money or materialism can give us this love. Love is here in the community, in the connection between people, between the earth and the food we eat, that was grown by a mother's hands. In every action in Nepal, I saw love. I am not sure why I never saw life like this before. I guess, like the Buddha, I had only seen one side of the coin. Love was in every action if you looked deep enough.

I noticed many Nepalese people touch their forehead and then the object in front of them. On this day, I witnessed Govin touch his head, then heart, three times whilst also touching his motorbike. I asked him why he did that. He told me it was to bless the bike and to connect with it.

'To get out of my head, into my heart, I am with the bike and we are one,' he said.

I loved this, grounded and connected instantly. The Nepalese recognised the energy that flows between and through all things, without even realising it. It is just a part of how they live.

Chapter 21
The Lotus

Is it possible to find clarity and simplicity in the mud?

Being on the motorbike through the mountains heading north in the central west to Baglung was one of the most freeing experiences in Nepal. The two-to-three-hour trip was always welcomed as it was an opportunity to go out into the real Nepal. Into the countryside, riding through villages, waving to the children playing on the side of the road or the women working on the farms. The views always ignited my creativity and, above all, my love for nature and life. I felt so free on that bike. It instantly connected me to life. I felt alive. In those moments, I felt so close to Govin, completely trusting him and aligning with him, the bike, the road and the environment. These are times I miss the most. I felt I could happily float away to heaven. I wanted and needed nothing in those moments.

In Baglung, I was always mindful of my intrusion as a foreigner and despite my efforts to blend in, even wearing clothes that don't clash with the culture, my presence still invited stares all round (Don't think I will ever get used to that). I understand that to see a foreigner in these parts was not a daily occurrence. After all, it is not every day they see a white girl with yellow hair wandering around the streets of Baglung.

Upon our arrival, we had headed to the Kali temple. Govin said that when he had been away for a long time, it was important to come back to the temple and give thanks and prayer. I found the idea of praying in this way was very public and within me arose the question: is prayer, devotion and meditation a private thing between your soul and the deity or place in which you are connecting or is it more powerful when connected with others sharing the same intention?

The idea of connecting feminine and masculine together, unifying consciousness, is a beautiful thing, no matter the tradition you choose to action this. I still feel we can connect directly to the source or god/goddess without the need for temples. However, I am open to the experience, so I try my best to be present and follow him in the devotion to Kali. After visiting the temple, Govin told me he always felt a little lighter and reconnected after the temple visit and I had to admit, so did I.

Watching the people touch their forehead and heart in acknowledging their gods and, for that moment, becoming one with all creation. Connecting head and heart, masculine and feminine, I observed the need for more of this type of practice everywhere in the world. I was enjoying exploring the Hindu traditions; I felt they had a lot to teach me, and I honestly noticed many small pieces of the puzzle in my mind coming together, forming a clearer picture about life and meaning. I was certainly receiving a lot of confirmation about my own inner truth. The gods and goddesses seemed to be so powerful and present in everyday life here that it was easy to see why people here had a different concept and expression of love.

Love and devotion were at the core of everything they did. The way they looked after their families, their friends and the respect that was present in so many of their actions. It was difficult to comprehend this without experiencing and being witness to it. I was truly in awe of it, still now. I feel this is missing from our modern life. We have lost reverence, grace, and connection with the divinity of life. We seem to not value our parents, our elders and our communities, and how as a collective unity we have more power, instead we separate everything, which creates powerlessness.

We all have a purpose, whether we are aware of it or not. We are born with a blueprint. Our DNA ensures we have everything we need for this lifetime. At certain times in our life, certain triggers will unlock the next level. If you like, think of it as a computer game with levels and goals to meet at each level. We have to achieve or experience certain things before we can access the next level or get the next tool necessary to move towards our goal or soul's purpose.

In Vedic traditions, this is called your dharma. We all have a dharma and it is linked to your DNA, your environment, your upbringing, your unique set of circumstances that enabled you to exist in this time. During my journey here, I was finally starting to understand and make sense of my dharma.

As a daughter of migrant parents from different corners of the globe, until recently, I had never pondered the reason I had often felt like a visitor in Australia. I had always felt like a visitor everywhere. I always felt like an explorer.

I had always had a global consciousness. My father's ancestors were from the Netherlands, Germany, Indonesia and China and my mothers were from the UK; it seemed I had roots all over the planet.

I love the countryside in Australia, its diversity and the freedoms of being an Australian are very much appreciated. Even if I see this changing at a rapid rate, with so much power being handed to corporations and governments to profit from anything and everything.

I have always been aware of the assault that the early migrants had on the precious eco system and Indigenous culture. Even as a child, I could feel the ancestors of the indigenous people restless and disturbed by the way people disrespected the land. I remember visiting places with my parents and feeling the immense sadness and despair, not really understanding at the time why, although now it makes sense to me. As an empath, I feel. For me energetically, I have never felt settled and at home here.

Five years ago, I visited outback Australia and I remember having the distinct feeling that I needed to ask permission to be there. I remembered feeling like I was being guided and spoken to. In special sacred Indigenous locations, I could feel the presence of the ancestors and they were showing me and allowing me to feel them.

To think of it now seems strange. I will never forget meditating at a gorge one day near Kings Canyon and feeling the energy of Albert Namatjira watching over me and speaking to me gently about Indigenous spirituality and the importance of not losing this wisdom, and how we needed to protect the knowledge before it was lost in time. Whether this was my imagination is not really relevant, the message is the same. We need to pay attention and respect our ancestors and what their culture can teach us about living.

As humans, I feel somewhere we have gotten a little off track and lost our connection with our planet and the reason is that we don't share our stories and wisdom anymore. We've forgotten how to connect with the amazing universe. We have become too much in our heads and forgotten our hearts. Respect is gone, especially for our elders.

My mother's parents were from England and my father's parents were from Netherlands and China and Indonesia. I was always fascinated by my roots. This became even more apparent as I spent time in Baglung with Govinda's family, born and raised in a culture that is thousands of years old, steeped in tradition. The roots there were so deep that it would be difficult for them to imagine another place as home.

We woke early the next day in Baglung and wound our way up the mountain to the terraced hill of rice paddies. The beauty of this location was amazing. Just being up there was so healing. There was something so organic that I could not quite put my finger on it. In every direction you could see mountains, clear skies, eagles and the feeling was so grounding. To sum it up, it really brought me back to earth. It was rice planting season, and I had this amazing reverence for these resilient people, their land, their ancestry and the traditions that had stood the test of time. High in the mountains, in tiered sections, there I was with my legs ankle deep in mud, planting rice. Witnessing the whole family coming together to grow their food was so surreal. There was so much blood, sweat and tears that went into this land and this rice, it was undoubtedly filled with love.

The stories and respect for their ancestors were so woven into life that for people in Nepal, there was no question about who they are and the role they are to play. The conflict arises as modern society makes its way into the younger generation, filling their heads up with capitalist ideas, which seem appealing at first. For many people there, it will create great conflict and ultimately more pressure. The fact of the matter is that the very idea of capitalism is not sustainable, it relies heavily on the individual journey, not a community's. So, the family connection is becoming more challenged as young Nepalis face conflict within themselves between supporting and respecting family and chasing money to make life better, to move out of poverty.

I guess the point I'm making is that somehow, we need to protect the culture and way of life here, or anywhere that culture is still intact, before it is lost completely.

There is so much to value in the traditions that make Nepal strong, resilient, and connected to universal wisdom; not to mention their ability to look at life through a positive lens despite the many hardships that is Nepali life. Many visitors that come here, look at Nepal through Westerner eyes and with this view, they will see many things that will conflict with what they think, is 'right'. The key to learning about any culture is to come as a blank slate. Just be in it, no judgment, observe, communicate and learn. I remember a foreigner saying she wanted to do a project that helped women get off the floor and cook in upright stoves. She felt she was doing a great thing for women. I asked my Nepali friend to explain to me why many Nepali women still prefer to cook in outside kitchens or on the floor. His reply was this: 'Women here have a choice, but they prefer to sit and cook. They grow up sitting on the floor squatting, they are used to and enjoy sitting by the fire on the floor cooking.' I observed many of the family often gather in this space too, to assist or just to talk. Nepali people love to talk. 'She cooks this way', he said 'because she finds standing up to cook, hard work and she gets pain in her legs and back.'

So, who are we to judge or decide that it's time for change? Nepali people will adapt and change in their own way in their own time. Change needs to be organic and come from a desire within. Something we have learned in Australia about forcing change amongst the Aboriginal people. It created such a loss of identity that many Indigenous Australians are so disconnected from their roots that they are struggling to live in modern Australia. They have not been allowed to evolve and change in an organic way. They have lost their stories and connection to the dreamtime. The importance of family ancestry and tribal connectedness is through storytelling.

Without storytelling, the culture dies, the people have no guidance or awareness of self and how they came to be. Sometimes, to know where you're going, you need to know where you have been.

The whole family gathered on the farm on this day to do their part. They told me it is a fun day, and they looked forward to it every year in the Monsoon season. I could feel and see the joy on their faces and actions whilst they worked. They'd start work at 7 a.m., clearing the rice field and making it ready for the buffalo to come down and move the soil, well, the mud. The water was flowing down the mountainside and flowed into the rice field, quickly making it muddy and wet. Later, I was told that the right time to plant was when the water was naturally flowing. The Nepalese work with the seasons and nature. The most amazing part of this experience was going barefoot in the mud. There was something so cleansing and earthy about getting my feet in the muddy water feeling truly connected to the earth. Feeling the textures, heat and cool and aligning myself with the seasons. Above all, there was no rush or urgency. It was a gentle process of hard work, with an organic smooth flow to it. I experienced such a sense of satisfaction and feeling of being whole and connected to the planet that I cannot do it justice with words. It is forever etched and recorded in my being.

After a few hours, it was time for the women to gather in the lower fields and pick the previous planting of rice, bundle it up and then, in a few hours it would be replanted and spread in the larger fields. So, I sat with the women and did my part. They were so used to sitting on the ground or squatting that for the ladies, this was the easiest, most relaxed part of the day. For me, I am lucky that I'm reasonably flexible, however my back did start to complain after two to three hours.

After the rice picking, we all gathered together for lunch. It was a beautiful sight; the women had all cooked earlier that day and everything, including pots and pans, plates, and all was brought up to the fields on their backs in baskets. It was a feast. Traditionally, of course, we ate dal bhat, although there was extra aachar made for me and roti bread, which they knew I enjoyed. Aachar is a vegetarian dish, usually with potato, garlic, lemon vinegar, spices and my fave, fried hemp seeds. I was in awe of the effort that went into this feast. Nobody went hungry, anyone nearby was welcomed.

I loved the way the women had prepared the lunch earlier and had trekked virtually the whole kitchen up the mountain to the rice farm to feed the family during the hard work. I found that eating like this really started to change my consciousness around food as fuel instead of food as a pleasure. The Nepali eat to refuel, they enjoy it, however it comes from a place of refuelling versus the western idea of food as pleasure and indulgence. Don't get me wrong, the taste of the dal bhat and Nepali food is amazing, but it's difficult for a Westerner like me to imagine eating the same thing every day, morning and night, which is how the Nepalese live.

After the lunch gathering, it was time for the real hard work! The men were busy with the buffalo, working hard in the mud, digging, harrowing and removing rocks. By this time, they were covered from head to foot in mud. To walk in the paddies, the mud comes up to your mid calves in some spots. Hard yakka indeed! The women got busy planting. Before long, I was in sync with these ladies and we were focused, all the while having fun and laughing. My kurta (traditional Nepali woman's clothes) which was clean when I started, soon became a grotty wet mess as I placed each rice plant deep into the mud. After several hours of songs, chiya (tea) and chappati? we finally finished, exhausted and satisfied with our achievements at 7 p.m.

It was getting dark as we drove down the mountain back to Baglung, a luxury that was afforded to me, whilst the others walked down, loaded up with the baskets of empty pots and pans. I think the family were surprised at how much I got involved and helped. Personally, I was in awe of them and realised just how sheltered a life I had lived. I felt a deep sense of connection with their way of life, myself, and the planet as we drove down the mountain balancing the baskets. It was one of the most natural and organic experiences of my life.

Chapter 22
Community – A Tribal View

How many people in life can say 'I lived', 'I lived fearlessly, whole heartedly, unafraid and gave my all'?

For most of us, living day to day is about survival. No matter where you live in the world, whether it is in Africa, the USA, Australia, China or Nepal, it is all relative. Our societies all function fundamentally in the same way. Security first, food, roof, a job, taking care of daily living and our families. If you were one of the millions born in a developed country, you also get the option to imagine, to chase your dreams unashamedly and I guess that is the big difference – something often named 'privilege'.

In Australia, we can dare to follow our dreams, we dare to take risks. We have a social structure that supports independence and allows us to take some risks. This doesn't mean we don't have poverty in Australia. We do. However, in the worst of situations, most people still have access to Social Security, healthcare and services, if they want it. Can you imagine what happens in a society that does not have social services structure or government support? After spending ten months in Nepal and immersing myself into their society as best as a white girl could, I learnt some things about why so many people here do not dream dreams. Why tomorrow is not planned for, why young girls are sometimes married off early, or worse still, sold, and why the emphasis is on family and supporting the extended family community is the responsibility of everyone. Independent thoughts are a luxury here. In a sense, I observed that Nepali culture is still quite tribal in its structure.

In a country where the government does not provide social security or the pension, and old age comes quickly because of the nutrition and hard life, it means that most Nepalis have a view that if they cannot make some money in their twenties, then they are destined for a life of poverty and struggle. Growing their own food predominately is one of the ways they manage to always feed their families. However, a fifty-year-old here is the equivalent to an eighty-year-old man in Australia. Who looks after you when you cannot work or grow your food? Your children. In a country where women are still mostly uneducated, it falls to the men to financially support their families. Women are the backbone of most families tending to the home. In this society, where electricity is not free flowing and electrical appliances do not exist, this is a full-time job, as well as a respected one.

Health care here is not subsidised and access is limited, especially in the villages. Many men die in their sixties, usually of liver and kidney diseases due to alcoholism or from diabetes and other heart related illnesses. I can't help but compare the issues in village life here as being very similar to the Indigenous people of Australia.

Family structure is so important here and the effect this has on an individual's ability to think for themselves or follow their dreams or even imagine an abundant life is almost unthinkable.

Of course, they desire to improve their financial situations, but the magnitude and overwhelm of how to do it is so big and lost in the day-to-day survival and living, and limited by their experience and exposure to the outside world. Even the more educated Nepalis who may seem to have a lot of time on their hands struggle with ideas or creating anything new because the whole system here is not based on creating, it is based on survival; it is risky to step out of the tribe.

Entrepreneurial thinking here is a relatively new concept and non-existent, in most places in Nepal. Many educated Nepali look around and see a country devoid of opportunity. There are no supports, government grants or traineeships.

Being a freethinker, or creative thinker here could change your life, but for most Nepali, it is so risky, especially with the caste issues that exist. 'Who will support me if I break from the pack...' mentality is something that will probably start to change now with the internet being available everywhere, however this presents a whole new set of issues. There is a freedom here though, that I don't think Nepali people who have never seen the world are aware of. I think I can see it because I have lived in Australia, and potentially now that Govin has lived here too, he can also visualise new opportunities for Nepal.

Let's be clear though, Australian life/ Western life has a whole different set of survival challenges; for example, struggling to pay bills and making ends meet and the conflict of wanting to chase big dreams, although stuck in the endless cycle of paying the bank to live in a country that operates through credit. One thing I noticed very quickly in Nepal is the simplicity that exists there. There is a 'connectedness' to each other, a common thread uniting them in their struggle. Something that I have never felt or experienced in my personal struggles in Australia. In Australia, struggle seems to be a hidden, and individual thing. We tend not to ask for help, we suffer in silence. We feel ashamed at not being able to do it ourselves. Nepalis have beautiful friendships and bonds with family, that despite the many issues that relationships incur, including infidelity, abuse, and illness, there is a loyalty, a level of support and care for their fellow Nepali. There is a 'we are all in this together mentality', and a sense of duty and responsibility to their kin, which keeps everyone connected at some level and responsible for each other.

I have witnessed more Nepali people involved in charities and community events and peer-to-peer lending money than I have ever seen in Australia. I have seen many Nepali people who have no job, no assets, give their last dollar to the homeless man on the street. It is so inbuilt in their psyche to give back to society and help others that it is inspiring me all the time. They are truly the original social funding gurus.

If your friend or family is in trouble, you help first, ask questions later. When a Nepali person says 'Dhanyabad' (thank you), they really mean it. They don't say it often, it is not like in Australia, it is only said when it is really felt deeply. Like many words we take for granted, like 'sorry', they only say them if they really mean it and are truly feeling the emotions of sorriness or gratitude. Here, if you don't take responsibility for your life or actions, you could end up hungry or out on the street. In Nepal, relationships are very important. They do not quit at the first sign of trouble. They are loyal, and when they love, they love deeply with an acceptance that love can be messy, ugly, challenging, and equally joyful and fulfilling. Their love seems to have purpose and they accept the totality of it. Here, family connectedness is everything. It is survival of the tribe and indirectly, survival of the self.

There is an unwritten understanding in Nepal of what the roles are in a family. It is clear and defined, there is no question about where each person sits in the family unit and what their role and responsibility is. Everybody respects the importance of their role and the purpose of it. For example, The father sits at the head of the family and the eldest brother soon becomes his deputy, because property is handed down through each generation. Families live close and the patriarchal lines are very clear. I have noticed when outsiders visit, they project their modern views on to the Nepali way of life, and in doing so, they do not always see the beautiful balance that exists within these families. The respect and the way they function. I feel that western society could learn a bit from experiencing and spending time in these cultures and experiencing how they work in reality.

A wife's role here is to support her husband and children, to take care of the home so that the husband can financially support the family. They all work together with a common goal of surviving and creating a harmonious home.

Now, to a foreigner, this may seem oppressive or disempowering, but that thinking is based on our modern upbringing of being independent women, we take our independence and individualism seriously. We have been educated to see the world as an equal opportunity. Whilst I see and have had the privilege of being a modern woman, I can also see the sacrifices and the effects it has had on the family unit, on relationships, our self-esteem and stress levels.

Women here take pride in their roles as homemaker and mother. It is without doubt the biggest job they could have. They do it with love, duty and care and I have met young women who express their preference to do this, rather than have a career. I remembered a story I was told by a member of the Bahini foundation. An opportunity was offered to some marginalised village women for a free education and training to become bakers, and eventually business owners. Despite the lucrative opportunity, they declined the offer. They felt there was more honour and pride in being a wife than being independent. For women here, if you are not married and have no family, it is not a sign of independence and strength, but the opposite.

To them, it was a sign of weakness and made them vulnerable. To be married in Nepal was a sign of success. Women and men who are not married worry about these things; Who will take care of you in your old age? And, if I am alone, there is something wrong with me. Not to be mistaken for 'lonely', what they mean is, what value is your life, if it is not sharing, supporting or giving with another person?

Marriage and family all centres around service. To me, this was interesting to contemplate. I could see the connection to many spiritual faiths that also advocate that service is the best way to connect and become one with God or have eternal peace. As much as this was the reality in Nepali villages I visited, life in Nepal is changing slowly, especially in the cities due to education, TV and the internet. I believe this change is likely to create considerable destruction and uncertainty in the traditional family unit and, without social support, we may see a lot of social problems in the future for Nepal. To be honest, I am already seeing this. It is important for women to grow and expand. However, the gap between the elders and the new generation is huge. It will be a tumultuous journey for these trail blazers as they break away from the tribal mentality and move toward modernity. I just hope they don't lose their culture and some beautiful parts of their family communities as a result of modernisation. As a mother myself who often struggled, due to the conflicting pressures of a transitioning modern society, to chase her dreams and be the perfect mother, I am very aware of the impact this is having on many modern mothers more than ever. In my view, marriage is a partnership and raising a family is a community responsibility. More than ever, we need to connect to our tribe. To be part of a tribe, a family, a culture is a beautiful thing and I think it is important at this time. It is human nature to be connected to other humans. Suffering is shared, and a burden shared is a burden halved. Not to mention the understanding and feeling of belonging that occurs, and bonds are strengthened through shared experiences. The support that allows us to fall apart and be human and recognise the strengths and weaknesses inherent in us all.

To witness another's life can be humbling and joyful as much as it can be challenging and cause suffering, but undoubtedly the most valued gift any of us could ever hope for. To walk alone in the world chasing dreams is not a guarantee of happiness. It has no purpose without service. What good is success if you cannot share it with others who have walked with you or understood the sacrifices you made or the challenges you faced? Or if you did not lift others up with you? Without purpose, roles and responsibilities, life can become an empty vessel of accolades and materialism that leaves us empty and disconnected from ourselves, each other, and the planet. Finding our tribe, our people, connecting and building our dreams together in common unity. Together we can create great change, not only in this country, but in the world.

Russell Brand, a popular comedian, turned spiritual/selfhelp guru of sorts, says, 'Organised collective, collaborative, contribution and togetherness to create common unity' – Community.

At this point in Nepal, I started to feel on purpose, connected, feeling like I had a role to play. I was realising the importance of my role. I was realising my worth as a mother and woman in a natural and organic way. Lastly, I was feeling blessed to have met this man who had opened my eyes to so much and new ways of seeing life. He expressed himself more clearly and openly than many men I'd met in my life, with an openness that constantly had me in awe. I had met a man who barely spoke English, yet he communicated beautifully. I wanted to support him, somebody who understood the importance of family and what real partnership looks like.

I was feeling transformed, healed, and part of something so new and expansive that I knew it was going to change my life forever. My perspectives flipped. Without expectation for the future and without judgement and ideals, I made a conscious choice to remain open, to continue, to learn and grow. I was looking forward to reconnecting with my own family in a new way when I went home, recognising the connectedness between us all. We are all family, and we are all part of a tribe.

Chapter 23
Kali Kaleidoscope, We Are in Relationship With Everything

I had needed to change my view for a long time; I had learnt that much about myself. I loved the ocean for that very reason. Every time you visit it, it looks a little different; it creates space for you to expand and move into. This was one of the biggest motivators for me to come to Nepal, the amazing views, as far from the ocean as you could get, but despite that, it had a similar pull for me and beckoned space.

I'd been in Nepal for around five months and around this time I had started to think fondly of Australia as well and the diversity that exists within our country in both the landscape and its people. This was one of the things I loved about Australia, its diversity. Yet we are often so busy earning an income that we don't get to enjoy the beauty and freedom of this country. Change and diversity are natural. It is the one constant that exists consistently throughout the whole of the universe. Whenever I think of these images, it makes me feel calm and insignificant in a healthy way, like I can relax and let go, because I am just another grain of sand. It takes the pressure off to be something or create something and sometimes we need this.

Goddess Kali is constantly preparing us for change, creation, and destruction. She is teaching us that to stay the same is death. Stagnation destruction, in which we have choice, either to be destroyed or to move, integrate and transcend and start creating again with a new downloaded upgrade. Either way, we will transform kicking and screaming, or willingly. We have to flow with change; we have to embrace change and allow for growth; it is nature and the way of life. To resist change is to suffer, and suffering leads to disease. Quite simple, really, yet so many of us find this so challenging.

Living in Nepal was certainly teaching me that, especially in the aftermath of the earthquake. Everyone was accepting and adjusting their view and embracing change. Nothing stays the same, not even our planet. I feel that when our view is fixed and does not change, then we stop growing, stop learning, stop expanding and stop seeing. It feels like a cluttered and foggy brain. Maybe part of the problem in our societies is that we have become so caught up in survival and living that we forget it is in our DNA to move about, to adjust, adapt, change and navigate the impacts of living on this ever-changing planet. We are nature. Yet we have become insulated and disconnected from all that we are.

Once upon a time, humans were nomads, constantly having to adjust and adapt to new environments, learning to respond to the diversity of the environment. Deep within my core, I have always had this desire to move about, to explore, uncover, seek and participate in something bigger and more expansive than day-today survival. I know it's not for everyone. I can appreciate that many of my friends enjoy the comforts of the familiar and their own homes. However, for me, this always feels so heavy. I am lightest and at my best when I'm exploring. Full of wonderment like a child, open, loving, and free. This is where I learn the most about myself and others. This is when I do my best work, my best learning.

I was feeling blessed, realising my dreams, and I was now choosing to acknowledge that I am a citizen of the globe, not just a country. Learning and playing in the world. I like living this way, a bit like a detective gathering intel. I had never valued things as much as I valued experiences, people, and places. I believe for us to evolve and truly become more connected at every level, including on a global level, we have a responsibility to learn about the world. I believe that everything that exists at this time, the internet, airplanes, cars, education is asking us to do this. We, as a human existence, dreamed this into being.

For as long as I can remember, I have not resonated with modern domestic lifestyles, seeking assets and materialistic things for security. It made me feel bogged down. I had never been truly motivated by money, I'd be more interested in what money could do and create, rather than what it can buy. My most treasured items are transport to take me anywhere, my guitar and laptop.

The space between love and fear is so small that it is easily overlooked. I mean, how often do we sit in fear, broken, depressed or overwhelmed, not realising that if we just look over our shoulder that love is there, waiting patiently, just sitting, wondering when we will see its endless support? I know this may be hard for some of you to accept, especially if you feel love has left you. I can relate to that feeling too. But with each experience, I have learnt to start seeing where the love is, and not to always focus on the perception of where it is not.

For a long time after my divorce, I started to think that maybe the reason I was not settled or could not feel connected to another person was because maybe I was different, maybe I was broken, or something was not right with me. I decided I needed to change my view, my perception of love, and decided that marriage was just a piece of paper that did not mean anything. I convinced myself I did not want it again or believed in it. It was an outdated notion that made people feel stuck and lifeless, is what I told myself. Funnily enough, I often watched other married couples in judgment, thinking how boring and disconnected they were and miserable. I convinced myself that is what marriage was.

I decided to focus on self-love and participated in many activities that made me feel good and distracted me from what was deep within, the need to be loved by another, to be connected to another and have another witness my life and me having the privilege to walk beside them and witness theirs.

I experienced many firsts and explored things that were amazing. There was nice freedom in being alone that I slowly got used to and I started to find that I would choose solitude in lieu of company. Slowly withdrawing and feeling disconnected from others further fuelled my intention to not want or need anyone, making me believe that I was happy alone. Was I just trying to convince myself? I was scared that maybe I would never find anyone that I felt at home with; I was scared of rejection.

There were one or two couples in my life who stirred something within me. No matter how I tried to see the negativity of their relationship, I also saw equally a positive and there was something that I envied about the connection they had. To find a word to describe this is difficult, but I think it is a mutual respect and that they equally complemented each other.

Both of them had equal power and energy in the relationship, which was delicately balanced by the respect they had for each other's roles in the relationship.

Coming to Nepal had opened my eyes to so many things, how much this country had impacted me and allowed me to see myself. In the past few years, I had realised how much I valued family, how much I had missed and wanted that connected feeling of belonging to my tribe. I realised how broken I was from my divorce and how much I'd suffered from the pain and loss of expectations, what I'd hoped for, and grieved for the loss of my family. I'd been wrestling with guilt and self-love for a long time. The strange thing was the only reason I was able to realise this was through the love of another. It seems the fastest way to selflove is to allow another to love you, broken, warts and all. This was harder than loving myself.

To accept that another can love you like that takes self-love to a new level. I was loveable, after all. It had taken so much courage to allow myself to be loved by another person other than my mother and father and love back that, I can see now, the line between fear and love is almost invisible, they are so close. I perceive that they are both love, just like the Yin and Yang. The culture in Nepal is so ingrained in the way of life that people here communicate their feelings. They are open, they are direct, and they share. People here understand reverence. Maybe it is a language thing, as the English language is so complex. We have so many words, we can talk around everything and in doing so, we can avoid feeling. We have become experts at it. Maybe that is why so much mental illness exists in our culture? Too much language, not enough feeling.

We can talk our way in or out of anything, because we spend so much time in our heads, rationalising and analysing. In comparison, the Nepali language is direct and straight to the point, it is feeling centred.

I had been denying half of myself by not allowing a mirror or being brave and vulnerable enough to look in the mirror. I had found my mirror, Govin.

OSHO, the spiritual guru, talks about this; that the true path to experience yourself and life is through relationships. Without having relationships, you are only seeing half or parts of yourself. We are made to complement each other perfectly so that we attract the perfect mirror to help us see and realise our feminine and masculine selves, to see the shadow self, the parts of ourselves we have yet to see or realise. To make conscious the parts of ourselves that are dormant. To activate or trigger the parts of ourselves, we need to integrate. In other words, we are triggered by relationships because we are designed that way. The trigger acts like a switch to turn our attention to the hidden part of you, so that you can bring it in to the light and learn how to use this new tool. Initially, it can feel very uncomfortable, and we often resist this change or experience by being reactive. However, once we surrender and understand the process and the amazing tools we can uncover through relationships and being challenged, we can understand better just how power-full we really are and what we are capable of.

Relationships are all around us, with each other, our partners, our kids, our friends and ultimately, the planet. We are in a relationship with everything.

Chapter 24
Truth

In most cases, when confronted with the truth, most of us find it extremely challenging or uncomfortable and will direct the conversation away from the depths of truth. We have built whole societies around hiding the truth. I believe that modern western life is all about hiding truth and giving people the illusion that they are in control of their lives and that everything is perfect.

I think this is one reason why, when confronted with the truth, so many people have breakdowns. They suffer from anxiety or depression because they have not been brought up in a society that embraces truth. Therefore, when we are forced to see a new truth so often our egos cannot handle the shattering of the belief system that has been comforting our own personal truths up to that moment and will fight or resist it. For the most part, we all have our own little versions of truth.

Absolute truth or universal truth are the things that are factual or cannot be argued. If it can be argued then it is only a matter of your truth or mine, not the 'actual' truth, and this is the problem for many cultures and religions and why wars are fought and people suffer. Whether we chase the universal or absolute truth consciously or sub-consciously, deep down when we hear the universal or absolute truth, we know it. It is a feeling, a resonance, like hitting the right note in a song. It cannot be denied. The truths we learn about ourselves offer us an opportunity to accept, grow and work with the energies and environment that we are in.

The truth can be ugly, it can also be extremely beautiful. The truth is a resonation, a knowing that everything is aligned in that moment. When you hear it, you feel it. Truth is felt in the deepest part of your soul, it is connected to your DNA, it has been recorded in our being from the beginning of time.

Many of us, in our efforts to avoid pain and hurt, hide from the truth, protect others from the truth, do our utmost to blanket the truth, not only in our own personal lives, but in our societies. Through the media, we are censored, and the truth is hidden. Governments hide the truth, globally we hide the truth. In this way we can trick ourselves into believing that we can keep it all nice and lovely, we are in control, we can protect our children from the reality of all the ugly things in the world, in this way we can avoid pain and hurt. Just look around you. Does it work to hide all the truth? Maybe temporarily, however, it has to be experienced at some point and I believe if hidden too long, it will erupt like a volcano, causing a wave of destruction. Like Buddha's father, protecting him from the truth, believed with all his heart that he was doing the right thing from a place of love. However, eventually Buddha needed to experience it and because he was denied for so long, it catapulted him into a journey of seeking it in a full immersive fashion.

I feel that in denying the truth we immediately disconnect; we create a gap in our psyche and ultimately unconsciously create an illusory bubble around ourselves. This starts happening early in life when our parents protect us from anything that may cause us any kind of disappointment or pain.

I believe we need to be guardians of our children and help them learn about their world through experiences that will empower and teach them about their world in a truthful, honest, and loving way. They need to learn that there is always balance and that we will have happy days and sad days. By not showing our children the truth and overprotecting them, we are creating a generation of children that will become anxious and depressed whenever they are confronted with challenges. We have a responsibility to cultivate a community that can navigate the waters of emotion, not hide from the waves or continuity of change.

When we deny the truth, we disconnect from others, the planet and nature, creating an emptiness, an insatiability resulting in greed, gluttony, and egoic behaviours. It encourages a complete disconnection from what it is to be a human on this planet, through constantly needing to drug, or placate ourselves with materialism or things that distract us and keep us satiated. This is the western way. So that we have mass consumerism, mental health issues and ever-increasing debt and stress.

Truth connects us, even through pain. A lie is about maintaining the status quo, it is about wanting to control a situation; it is manipulation and prevents growth and change. To know the truth is real kindness, real authenticity, real love without judgment.

'The truth will always come out,' my mother would always say, and she was right. It does, whether or not we are prepared or ready for it. You can never really be ready for the truth, it is uncertainty, its whole purpose is to create growth forcing us into faith and change, bringing us closer to our authenticity and of course challenging us to be more and choose a new way of being.

Living in Nepal, I noticed how much truth is hidden from us in Australia. In Nepal, you will see the homeless, you will see the poverty, you will see the disabled, rubbish, the dirt and all the ugly sides of being human, you see suffering and hardship. Yet in equal measure you see the beauty too, in humans helping each other, in the environment, the freedom in their lives, the smiles, the communities, the children, playing with nothing but joy in their hearts to be alive and much more. Truth is balance. It is seeing both sides of the coin. It is awareness of the polarity and duality of living on this planet. It is brilliant and teaches us about the 'wholeness' of our existence. It will shove us, move us, push us and get us to feel. It is only when we experience this depth of feeling that we belong to something greater, catapulting us to become motivated to contribute and connect to the planet fully, warts and all.

The truth leads us to an acceptance that helps us see perfection in the imperfection. It is reality in its purest and when we understand this, we can face adversity, we become resourceful; we are nature and nature is us. We can consciously change and create, harmoniously working alongside each other and integrating everything we learn.

'Every child has known god, Not the god of names, Not the god of don'ts, Not the god who never does anything weird, But the god who knows only four words and keeps repeating them, saying: Come Dance with Me.'

HAFIZ

Chapter 25
In the Darkness There is Always Light

Trying to make sense of life when you are in the middle of it is like trying to read a book without opening the pages, wanting to know the ending of a movie before watching it unfold on the big screen. Plain crazy to think one can experience life and understand what the experience is about or what it is teaching us at the same time. I can now see this is practical, as we could experience nothing fully and in the moment if we knew the whys and hows, I think removing the uncertainty and mystery removes the magic and makes life mundane. We have just lost touch with navigating and being okay with uncertainty. Life is a series of events and experiences that shape us and create who we are; always ebbing and flowing, oscillating between positive and negative, two forces pushing and pulling us to move, change and grow. The part I dislike about this sometimes is when I forget that my reaction to something is from my past and that I am being triggered to shift and look at my belief systems. I am stubborn by nature, so prefer to do it on my terms, however the universe loves to challenge this. Awareness is a funny thing and even though I might realise midway through the experience that I am being triggered, sometimes I still can't stop the reaction. Sometimes if I am lucky, I can catch the trigger and stop, breathe, and change the way I am handling a situation. A bit like being in a lucid dream when you suddenly become aware that you can manifest a sword and slay the dragon instead of running from it. However, even though the awareness comes, it can be very hard to shake yourself free of the destructive thought patterns that have been running in your mind without restraint for a long time in the past.

In Govin's village, his old aunty lives next door. She has dementia. In the past few years, her life has become very hard. Her daughter-in-law-left the house after taking out a stack of loans against it and the son is stuck in Dubai working hard to pay them back. She lives alone, and some days forgets to eat. However, every day Govin's family check in on her, feed her, take care of her home and help her in any way they can. Her grandson is taken care of by another local family and together, they all support her. Interestingly, despite the poverty in Nepal, most people belong to a family and families stay together and support each other, living together for generations. People in Nepal seemed to deal with sadness, grief, and loss in a much more matter-of-fact way. They accepted it was part of life, as was death. They understand the ebbing and flowing of all things, especially relationships. They seem to accept imperfections, and because of that, find it easier to find happiness.

Somewhere out there, when I left the crystal castle of my childhood, I got lost. I forgot how to be. Children are free, exploring their world uninhibited and full of acceptance and love. A child can play with another child and be so full of joy and love and not even know the child's name and or worry about if they will ever see that child again. Whilst they are playing, time is eternal and there are no thoughts of the future or past, complete presence, pure bliss, and joy. It might explain why I would often get into trouble for coming home late or for forgetting the time, as it was easy for me to be in this space when I was young. Time is long when you're a child. This feeling returned a little being in Nepal and having these new experiences. I was coming home somehow, coming back to that place of freedom and space like when I was a child. Full of awe and wonderment, the burdens and heaviness of the previous chapter of my life lifted, and I started to let go… Coming home to myself, slowing the pace down, learning what was important and who was important to me.

As an energetic being, I can easily move from the past to the future and back again; it is as easy as flipping a coin. I've had to learn how to manage this over the years. As a young person and in my previous marriage, I was often perceived as flippant and flaky because of this. I have now embraced this part of myself and recognise the ability to embrace change, be flexible and allow expansion is a gift. I can now see that being able to change, move, flex and bend is actually the very thing we need to be in this world and not suffer, instead of narrowing and stretching the view so far ahead as to leave no room for any other manifestation other than the point of fixation. If you imagine looking at a long straight road ahead and it slowly gets smaller until it narrows into point and disappears into the horizon. The largest part of the road with the biggest vision and most choices is right here in front of you, where the car is. You can't know what is ahead of you until you get further along the road. All you can navigate is this place. All the possibilities exist right there in the present.

This is one reason dance is so meditative for me. It allows me to move energy and all that pent up frustration, blocks and anxieties out of my body. It brings me to the present, into my body, into the space I occupy as I move my body and allow my soul to follow and flow with the music. Music allows the soul to journey without fixation, if we allow the flow. It is so healing and so primal. In all cultures, dance and music is a pivotal part of culture and storytelling. I remember the women in Nepal gathering during the Teej Festival time to celebrate, share stories and memories through dance and song. They sat around with acoustic djembes and drummed away whilst ad-libbing, rhyming, and battling in a circle with tales of daily life such as their sorrow, woes, and joys. Similar to rap artists doing a rap battle.

I'd sit in awe and sometimes dance too as they continued the beating and singing for hours.

These days I dance in my home with my music and just let go. It is a great way to connect and let go. This was something my meditation teacher in Pokhara, Nepal, confirmed to me when in the middle of meditation he turned the music up so loud and told us all to get up and dance! Such amazing energy followed, and then laughter. The energy we experienced and tingles through bodies after that session was amazing. We were so energised and buzzing.

Sometimes we can have the best of intentions. I came back to Nepal in 2015 to do more relief work and give my heart and soul, or so I thought. A judgment, perhaps? I mean, how arrogant of me to think that 'I' could come here and help these people. Did they need it? Do they want it? It was interesting to me how often we feel so much guilt as citizens from developed countries when we visit places like Nepal that all we think to do is help or give money. Never stopping to ask or think, maybe we need the help? Maybe there is something we need to learn from them? I mean, have you ever stopped and wondered how you would survive in Australia if there was an earthquake and it destroyed our power, deprived us of our petrol and our homes and buildings were destroyed? Hmmmm, it is something we don't often think about. But I guarantee you we would seriously be in a predicament, and I am not sure if we would handle it with as much grace and resilience as the Nepali people.

Many of us are without even the basic knowledge of how to cook from scratch, how to grow food, how to kill a beast, how to build shelter, how to be resourceful, and without fuel and power. Then what? What I've learnt from Nepal and the people there is that I need them more than they need me.

There was so much to learn from the Nepalese people, the way they think, the way they live, and function as a society. I became fascinated a little more every day at the resilience and resourcefulness. The support the Nepalese showed one another and their ability to cope with negligent governments and natural disasters inspired me. Every day, I felt more like a child on this planet who knew absolutely nothing. Every day I was surrounded by the most open and loving people that I'd ever met, despite the adversity and difficulties they faced daily.

I believe that one of the most powerful ways to learn is through sharing of knowledge, through sharing experiences. We can learn so much from each other, swapping knowledge and sharing cultures and finding new ways to build better communities and homes. The helping professions are fast becoming part of the biggest industry in the world, so we need to become conscious of how we are doing this and what our motivation is. Otherwise, we are manipulating and directing things to suit our own agendas.

What we want for someone else is always our issue or subconscious trying to come into the light, and it is important to understand this.

Communication combined with consciousness, compassion and the ability to be humble is key in helping, expanding our consciousness to encompass new ways to live in the world. There is so much more to learn about our world from each other, from other cultures, from different experiences and ways of life.

We need to see the gifts that are available from the experience of immersing ourselves in the world of others. Through doing this, we can experience the culture or situation in its entirety with no outside judgment or projection. We can do so much more as individuals supporting each other with compassion and kindness in everyday actions than we can by throwing money at problems. Much of the volunteer experience is intentionally good. However, the person who is participating can enjoy the inflation of their ego when in a position of power and control, and it becomes more of a business than real validation and helping. This is why I feel it is so important for us to cross culturally share, rather than volunteering and projecting our views, needs, emotions on others. Take the time to learn about others and what the community and people really need. Not what 'we' think they need.

Chapter 26
Life is Long…

I often heard Nepali people saying, 'life is long', which often puzzled me, because the average life expectancy in Nepal is around sixty-five years old. People in Nepal age quickly, and it is still surprising to me when I meet other women or men my age, that they seem ten to fifteen years older. Nepali people are not in a hurry. They always seem to have so much time and space to do things, there is never urgency or stress of speed. There is an acceptance of life and death, almost a surrendering to work with the environment and life here. Nepali people believe they have a small window of opportunity to make money and 'settle their life', as they put it. Which is why so many of them marry young and have children so young. They believe that after thirty-five, the opportunity to make money is gone. So they often try to get student visas to other western countries to work to improve their financial situation.

As soon as Nepali people finish school, they start to look at marriage. In their eyes, they will be old at thirty-five, and definitely by forty, and by then, they will be considering semi-retirement. Many agencies are making money, sending Nepali people overseas to study or work, tempting them with opportunities and money. This often means a life separated from family, wives or husbands, and this can create conflict within the individual for multiple reasons. For a young Nepali, this feels like a dream come true to go to the USA, Australia or Europe, however the reality of this is much different. The cost of living for Nepali people in these countries puts a lot of pressure on these families. Sometimes they can be abroad for over ten years trying to get ahead, sending money home to Nepal, to the wife and children, and barely saving enough to visit the family. It is a sacrifice many of them make, thinking it is the answer to their poverty cycle.

My friend Sudip is one of these guys, trying his hardest to make it in the USA. It is difficult to make ends meet, even with family support, he says.

As the cost of living is high, and he has to work ridiculously long, late night shifts to just barely cover the costs of his education. He misses his home so much and often takes to drinking just to get through.

Another friend of my husband is travelling to Poland, and in his desperation to settle his life, he ran away to marry his girlfriend just weeks before he left Nepal for Poland. He was worried that if he got stuck there for many years, that she would not wait for him and marry someone else.

The sad part is so many young Nepali men from the villages feel it is their only option to get anywhere in life.

Govin's uncle has been living in Dubai for over ten years and has been home only two to three times to see his wife and son, and all his earnings go to keep the roof over their heads.

And the ones that go and come back often suffer from depression because of the massive contrast in developed countries and their homes. Often feeling like they don't belong in either country. Sadly, I worry that this growing trend will slowly destroy the cultural traditions and way of life in Nepal. I agree Nepal needs developing, but it concerns me that the current pathway to doing that is more of a sacrificial one.

After spending time with the Nepali people and exploring Nepali life, I now understand what they mean by 'life is long'. Everything in Nepal goes slower. Life here is slow, everything happens at a pace that is determined by the environment, weather and logistics. Nobody is in a hurry here. I miss the words 'bistaari bistaari', which means 'slowly, slowly'.

Govin will often remind me of this in the kitchen, and I am brought back to the present, aware of the habit I have from living in a modern society of doing things so fast. I had been missing so many of life's pleasures at that speed; I didn't feel the wholeness of anything. I was fearful of feeling. I didn't notice the colours, the smells, the tastes, and the small joys.

I had noticed that when Govin ate, he would be very slow and not talk much, savouring every part of the meal. So I asked him, 'Why are you so serious when you are eating, you don't talk much?'

At first he said, 'Talking whilst eating is dangerous, I could choke on my food'.

I laughed and said, 'Well you can breathe between mouthfuls and chat.'

Then quietly he turned to me and said, 'Don't you want to taste every mouthful and enjoy your food? Taste the love in the food?'

One way that Nepalese wives and mothers express their love, respect and care is through feeding their men, children and wider community. I had been aware of this, but to hear him acknowledge that as well was a whole other level. I mean, to recognise that love in the food was equally respectful, loving and caring. I was instantly silenced and grounded in that moment. He showed me how to be present and truly feel.

In Ayurvedic medicine, they talk about the need to chew thoroughly and about being present with the food, allowing your body to digest properly and be satiated appropriately. For whatever reason, he was taught to eat this way. I could not debate the obvious benefits. Putting love and nourishment in your mouth seemed like a much healthier concept than taste or the subconscious deciphering whether food is good or bad. Perhaps that's why obesity in this country is not a thing. Being a little fat in Nepal meant you were healthy, content and loved. I learnt every day how to 'be more' and 'do less'. It wasn't easy to adjust to doing less for someone like me who was so used to juggling and running around multi-tasking after four children and the pressure of modern parenting and Australian life.

I noticed how much better my body was, despite so much of my mind struggling to slow down. After twelve months of Nepali influence and love in my food, I noticed I lost about ten kilograms. For me, this was unexpected and certainly was not something I was aiming for. Mostly, I was eating whatever I intuitively felt to eat or what was prepared for me. I still put it down to the way of life and less stress, because as soon as I returned to Australia, I quickly put it back on.

One thing I had noticed about myself was that if my mind was not busy, I had a habit of thinking about the future and falling into old patterns of thinking and worrying about negative things; 'what ifs', I call them. Being that life was slower there, I could catch the destructive thoughts before they took hold, this allowed me more space to make better choices and I found I operated less from a reactive space and more from a place that is aligned with love and nurturing for my soul. I started channelling this energy into actions that involved my body. I learnt that by doing this, I moved the destructive energy and focused it in a creative and positive way, through dance, walking and yoga and if the action activities failed, I wrote. Because in Nepal, life was slow enough that I had space to create these things because I felt like doing, rather than cramming them into small spaces of forced time, in between busy schedules.

So much of our reality is experienced in the past or future, causing us so much anxiety or depression. The mind likes to make sense of everything, a bit like trying to figure out where to store it in the filing cabinet – under 'R' for rational or under 'I' for irrational. It loves to think in black and white, right and wrong, because this is how it can form belief systems that will keep us safe from fear or pain. That is the ego at work. When we bring the mind in to the present, it can do nothing other than feel, observe and experience. This moment is when the heart is running the show and the mind is in a being state or servant's role.

I feel that because modern societies are moving so fast, with so much stimulation, I am not always aware of my thoughts and therefore, they escape easily, creating havoc in my life. I think this is true for many of us. Rippling out unconsciously, manifesting the very thing we are trying to avoid, always living in the past or future, trying to make sense of, or prepare for, the future. I had been following a fellow journeyman on Facebook, Dave. Dave was creating a wave of motion through his 'movement' series online. Dave was advocating movement as a way of being healthy, anywhere, anytime, anyhow. I loved it. It was so in sync with what was natural to me, and I felt I needed to embrace playful action more. I needed to recognise the power of movement, the joy of moving energy in a positive and creative way. This was another part of the mental health puzzle. The need for speed needs to change, I needed to slow it down. Movement did not need to be fast or competitive, it just needed to be enjoyable, freeing, expansive, creative and playful.

In this way, I engaged the mind to connect with the physical body and the physical environment. Connecting me with the planet as much as with myself with intention and focus, this grounded me every time. From this space, I naturally wanted to be more compassionate, forgiving myself, others, and the planet. It was the most natural thing to do to integrate mind, body, and soul. Try it sometime. Walk, dance, play barefoot, and feel your soul connect to the earth and creation.

Chapter 27
Like a Bird

Govin and I loved going for a ride on the motorbike around Fewa taal, (the lake) OMG I LOVED RIDING THAT BIKE. In fact, that is one of the things I miss the most!

One day we stopped to watch the paragliders, and this got me thinking. Max, my eldest son, was doing a paragliding course in India and he could easily make this his way of earning a living in the future. I am sure many people could not comprehend that as a job, but I was encouraging my children to think differently and instead of seeing limitations, to look for opportunities to create the lifestyle they wanted.

'It is never about the money.' I told them. It is always about the value of what you are doing for you and others. These days, I think we are too busy thinking about what career we want instead of learning about what lifestyle we want, or more accurately, what our dharma is.

After experiencing a large home versus a small home, I'd choose a small home. After having a new car versus a second-hand car, I'd choose the second-hand car. For me, a car is nothing more than a tool to get you from A to B. If it is reliable and does the job, then why spend $100,000 when I could spend $10,000? And then I could use my money for other lifestyle choices. If we are not living in accordance with what we value, if we are not living in harmony with our thoughts, actions, and words, then we will never find inner peace and contentment. By focusing on the things I was gifted at, my passions and joys, I found my purpose. Always do what you love, be what you love, Be LOVE. Conscious, Creative, Connected, Contribution, the four Cs. For me, they underpin everything I do. If these things are not woven through what I am doing, I will find it very difficult to stay focused and give it my all. So many people these days make the mistake of trying to 'be enough', or choose things that align themselves with others, or about fitting in with the Joneses, or pleasing others, then actually doing what they really enjoy and make their heart sing. Ideally, if I am living with my dharma, I am growing, expanding, evolving, and contributing. When I started living this way, it became so clear, and my life has become so much less cluttered. I am a huge advocate for experiences over things, as you have probably noticed by now from reading this. Often people push so much to have careers, chase financial freedom etc, but don't often stop to look at what really motivates or inspires them, and then wonder why they are never satisfied or why they can never rest. When living with your dharma you may get tired from working hard, however it is a different tired. It is the satisfying kind that fuels and re-energises you to go again the next day. Paragliders choose a way of life that allows them freedom, travel and enough money to do what they love. Maybe it's not forever, but it is a chapter in their lives that will most likely allow them to see the world and meet many people, whilst experiencing their passion for flying like a bird.

Whilst watching the paragliders, which is a mesmerising and meditative experience, I noticed a Nepali man fishing in the lake. It was so quiet and so peaceful that I had a moment; I breathed and realised that we take so much from the world, quite often more than we need. The little fishing boat was made of timber and he was just catching his meal for the day, not taking more than he would eat, with minimal impact on his environment. He seemed at peace, content with his actions in the knowing he would fulfil his dharma today and feed his family healthy fish. It was so peaceful watching him go about this task that I realised how much we have lost respect for so many things in this world. We take so much more than we need; we waste so much and consume even more. We are so separate from our environment that we buy packaged food and forget that at one time, it was breathing the same oxygen as us. We don't see the trauma or brutality of mass farming and go about our BBQs without blinking an eyelid for the beasts that sacrificed themselves so that we can feast and be a part of the tribe. We need to become more conscious about how we go about this process. As the saying goes, teach a man to fish... This is more true now than ever before, and I find it hilarious that so many NGOs will use this analogy about how they go about their business in helping. Yet I often ponder; how many of these workers they send to 'educate' the villagers can feed themselves, let alone catch their own fish? The man I saw that day was the richest man I'd seen for a while, living off the land as nature intended, fulfilled and content about his achievement for the day.

In Australian culture, I often feel that people think they are owed respect, they expect it or demand it from each other. I have even heard people say it's a dog-eat-dog world; got to look after me first. Govin says respect is given, always first. With every Tikka, every gesture in Nepal, there is a level of respect offered to the recipient. There is an understanding and appreciation of respect offered to the other person in a way that says, 'I can never know your journey, however I respect that you have walked it, and I have not, therefore, I cannot judge'. Namaste encompasses this, and this is a feeling and observation I have witnessed everywhere in Nepal. I remember the moment I dropped a book on the ground and Govin picked it up quickly, touching his forehead, chest and the book, and muttering to me that I was disrespecting the book by doing this. At first, I was laughing, but then I saw it. I saw what he meant; it was about more than the physicality of the book. The book just represented it. He was revering the creative source (God flowing through the hand of the human that wrote it) that created this book. The same source that exists in everything, including us. And to disrespect the book is to disrespect creation. It was this realisation that made me see just how much humans have disconnected from the source, God, ourselves, the planet, and what I needed to get back to. It is one thing to learn something by seeing it written, but quite another to experience it in this way.

The word 'Namaste' means to see in another the divine source which is also in you. This is the first word out of Nepali's mouths when they meet anybody. From books, to guitars, to animals, to people, I am learning to see more than just a material or physical thing, but an energy that exists within the objects and it permeates everything. Somebody or something has put time, energy and potentially love into this object. We all come from the same source. This source is to be respected and a physical thing that has been created, so that we don't take more than we need and that which we take, we respect and revere with gratitude. The red Tikka you see on many Nepali's foreheads is about that 'respect'. Respect is given first in Nepal. Reverence is real and practiced in everyday life. It is just part of who the Nepalese are.

Nepal grounded me. It showed me a reality that allowed me to be okay with me, to be okay with many things. It was like it ripped open the curtains that hide all the ugliness of life. In Nepal, I saw goats get slaughtered for food and nothing was wasted; I saw women and men working hard on the rice farms and labouring. I saw the street kids begging, and I saw people being raw and vulnerable. These things are not hidden from you. For me, this was so beautiful because I no longer felt like I was being hidden from the truth of life. I was seeing the totality.

Of course, many of us do not like seeing these things because it is the ugly side of humanity, so the developed world works on hiding these things. Old people are put out of sight, disabled people are put into disabled schools and homes, the rubbish is collected so we are in the illusion there is less. But in reality, we make more rubbish; it is just hidden from our eyes, so we can conveniently go about our day without the ugliness of our consumerism. Our capitalist society continues to rape the land and exploit people without us being too aware of it. It banks on our ignorance and the psychology of most people, not wanting to accept or see reality, always aiming to avoid suffering. Think about it, if it was not for the internet and social media, would we be so aware globally? We are more globally aware than ever, and that is how change happens, collective consciousness in motion. If we allow ourselves to see beyond the surface, if we allow ourselves, we can see that there is an opportunity for compassion and healing through seeing reality and not having it hidden from us. It allows us all to be real and would entice us all to be kinder, more productive people with purpose and certainly more community orientated. It also means we have a responsibility and cannot remain ignorant.

I found that by hiding the dark side of life out there. I was hiding the dark parts of myself, and I struggled to accept my perceived imperfections and often was my own worst judge and jury.

For me, seeing truth and reality was making peace with it. It helped me make peace with myself, because I could take action and be the change I wanted to see in the world and live a purposeful life. I could be honest with myself because I was surrounded by authenticity.

By avoiding pain, I avoided half of myself and lived half a life. So that when I was confronted with strong feelings or harsh realities, I was so overwhelmed by this, sometimes not able to even label what the feeling was, I'd drop my bundle, thinking there was something wrong with me or that I was weak. I'd start looking for answers and seek counsel from everywhere but inside myself. Eventually falling into a pit of despair, questioning what the purpose of my life was and even contemplating what it might look like if I did not exist. I did not want to see the ugly side of life. I avoided it at all costs. Yet here I was in Nepal, seeing the truth of it, and this was healing.

It was interesting, when I observed the resilience of the Nepali people and their strength no matter the obstacle, they seemed to have the ability to accept and overcome, through grace. However, in equal measure, they were vulnerable and fragile. Living in this part of the world showed me the power of accepting the imperfect stuff. I allowed myself to be imperfect. I allowed myself to be vulnerable and ultimately allowed myself to feel. I realised that to expand and grow, I had to feel; I had to allow both positive and negative in equal measure.

The shadow was as important as the light. The universe is perfect that way. This was Goddess Kali once more and the lessons she had for me. To be vulnerable, allowing love in all its forms to flow through me.

Chapter 28
Teej, Celebrating the Goddess and Her God

Traditionally, Teej is a festival to honour the Goddess Parvati and her marriage to Lord Shiva. After marriage, Shiva realised Parvati missed her family, and so he created an opportunity for the goddess to visit her home and family every year in Badhau (Sept/Oct). Hindus have since continued this tradition.

The women travel home to their families and spend time there, resting and sharing their stories of married life with their family. They sing songs and share the hardships of living away from their families and enjoy the dancing and festivities. In Nepal, when women marry, it is their duty to move to the husband's village and ultimately become the new head of the house. The woman's role is to look after all the duties in and around the home and take care of the children and ageing parents. Often in the beginning, it is a hard transition for them, resulting in many tears and conflicts between the mother and daughter-inlaw. Every year, the Teej festival is welcomed by women as an opportunity to sit together with their families and share their lives.

The festival lasts for three days and involves fasting for a day, lots of dancing, feasting (the men usually preparing the food and celebrations) and dressing up in their finest Saris, usually red and green as these are the colours that represent the marriage and union with Shiva. The fasting was seen as not only as a respectful action towards Lord Shiva, but also a cleansing act that is good for health. A big part of Hindu culture is based on purity/impurity, so it is relative to this that they fast to cleanse themselves in honour of Lord Shiva and their husbands for a long life. These days many younger women are embracing the idea that Teej is an opportunity to celebrate being a woman and they are certainly doing this, with Teej parties happening everywhere in Nepal. Women spend many rupees dressing up in their finest saris and luga. The beautiful colours and jewels are flowing and swirling at parties, on the streets and on the back of motorbikes as they enjoy and celebrate their inner goddesses. A mixture of young and old, no men allowed in these sacred parties as they are a woman only affair. It is interesting that they go to so much trouble to look so beautiful and amazing for each other and not men on this day. Dancing to a mixture of traditional songs and pop songs, sharing food together, chatting and celebrating the goddess.

At this time, they also walk together to the nearest Lord Shiva temple, taking offerings of rice, coconut, fruit and flowers and offer prayer for their husbands or significant men in their life, for long life and good health. It is lovely to watch them in all their beautiful colours, walking to the temple, a smiling and chatting rainbow of colour.

Spending time in Baglung at that time was so colourful and full of new experiences. Govin and I visited his family at this time because mine was too far away in Australia. When we arrived, he was immediately busy, as he was involved with a community group in his village that was active in creating social events for the village. It was nice to watch him busy and involved in his community in this way. So respected by his peers. I enjoyed meeting many of the locals and slowly practiced my Nepali. On the second day, I was invited onto the stage of the Teej event as a special guest, so nerve-racking and such a strange experience. In Nepal they honour guests in a big way, they revere them.

This was a new experience for me, and I was so uncomfortable dressed in my sari and on this rickety stage with about thirty other special guests and significant people in the community. I became aware of the guilty feeling and not feeling worthy of such respect as I felt I had done nothing to deserve this. For them, the simple fact that I was a visitor was enough to make me special. After my initial uncomfortableness about being raised above the people, I accepted and embraced the Nepali way of doing these things and soon became mesmerised by the process and the work the community group had put in to create this event for their community. There were performances from dancers, singers and comedians, and despite the lengthy talks by wannabe politicians and significant community members and the humid heat, it was enjoyable.

Towards the end, we were invited to dance on the stage and all of us danced so much that sweat was dripping everywhere, however it was so much fun. The one thing I noticed was that boys don't really dance with girls here. Such a new experience for me, growing up in Australia, predominantly dancing as a young person at the local football functions or pubs. The Nepali danced in circles around each other and often their actions matched the songs, although I certainly could not figure out what they were about. Probably all about love.

Every time I asked Govin what a song was about, he always answered the same way, 'It's about love baby'. Again, the rainbows of beautiful colours and all the people in the crowd were swirling, twirling, dancing, and singing along. I felt like I was in a dreamland entranced by the beautiful colours and joy amongst the people.

During the day, the community group ran some events such as shotput, slow race motorbike and the locals all got involved. Govin was so busy during those few days organising and helping his community with this event that I really was in awe of him and his mates for the brilliant effort they went to in providing their community with this entertainment. They took it very seriously and considered it their responsibility.

It was obvious at this event that women in Nepal are strong and revered, have opinions, desires and go about getting them met. The role they play in their communities significant, often the glue of the family and providing their husbands a place to rest after working and providing for the family.

Women here respect and take pride in their roles. They want to be good at being a wife and mother. Some may also have other dreams and no doubt, as education increases, then so will their desires and dreams expand. However, I am nervous that with this inevitable development that they do not lose this amazing resilience and pride in their most natural and instinctual roles. I believe it is most important that we do not remove the womanness in our desire for equality and or development. I think that now more than ever we cannot undervalue the role of women in the family, and the important part they play in raising our children and keeping families together and functioning. It's a fine line we walk in liberating supposedly oppressed women and supporting and lifting up something that already exists to be respected and revered in a whole new way. Maybe the tribal communities can teach us about being women and revering women after all.

We need women to band together to support each other; as they say, it takes a village to raise a child. Let's not undervalue the amazing job women are doing all over the world.

We don't need to modernise them to stop oppression; we need to educate people about the value of the roles they play.

Chapter 29
Union

Govin and I visited his family in Baglung to prepare for the official ceremony of our marriage. I was guided by him, as I was totally aware by now of the complicated depth of Hindu ceremony and tradition. Upon our arrival, there seemed to be more of a buzz than usual, as the family had supported our union, which was unusual in these parts for Hindu people to marry outside of their religion or culture. Govin's family always saw him as different to the others and I was aware of the way his mother had sacrificed so much to give him every opportunity to learn and become something.

I had watched and chatted with her many times by now in our broken Nepali/English and it was clear to me this woman had a special heart, like her son. She was smart, despite her literacy levels, and she knew how to maximise her opportunities within her ability and what was available to her. She would also regularly seek counsel from the local shaman/ healer. Ama (Sanu Ama) as she was known to me, meaning mother in Nepali, would talk endlessly with me and despite our language barrier our deepest conversations happened without words. The strength of this woman was beyond words, as I watched her tirelessly take care of the family home, cooking, cleaning, farming and preparing. She was truly an inspiration and to me, everything that a mother is. She had sacrificed everything for her children and to serve her husband and family. Govin had shared with me she had worked two jobs just to get him through school and university.

Govin's family was extremely poor, however despite their status in the village, Govin's mother was determined to rise above this. I could see this in how she had raised her children. They took a lot of pride in their appearance and in their responsibility to each other and the greater community. They were a unique family. Govin's father married his first wife and after years of trying to have children, it was learned that she was unable, so in true Nepali style he took another wife. His first wife even chose the new wife and introduced them.

To outsiders this would seem strange, yet here in this village it was perfectly arranged. Both women took care of the home. Thulo Ama (or big mother/first mother as she was known) took care of the father and of the bigger issues, and Sanu Ama (small or second mother) took care of the children. They had four children and lost the third one due to dysentery. They all lived together, and the aunty lived down the street; she had raised Govin's brother to make it easier on the family, when Govin's father was in India. The family would share Aunty's toilet as they did not have running water or toilet facilities in Govin's home. Govin had a hard childhood, no electricity, and sometimes food was scarce, however his ability to adapt, grow and evolve through this, is amazing to me. Despite the caste system being abolished years before, unfortunately it is still a big part of Nepali life, as one of the first questions out of Nepali people's mouths is 'what caste are you?' or 'what is your last name?'. Many times I witnessed this, and after speaking to Govin about it, I realised the only reason it still exists is because in this poor nation, it is one way people can feel better than their neighbour. I guess this was the ugly side of Nepal and humanity. The Brahman caste at the top benefit from being in a position of power so it serves them to keep following this system.

Meeting with the family and sharing our hopes for the future brought much excitement, of course, and no doubt the family felt their prayers had been answered for their 'special son'. For them, it meant security in their old age, which was a big concern for the people as there is no social security system and certainly no pension. Ama asked all about my birth date and then visited the shaman the next day and arrived home with our marriage ceremony date. Apparently, only the Shaman knows which date is best for our success. The date was set for October 4, 2015, and we set about arranging the day.

It was so strange for me as a western woman watching Govin organise the whole affair; it was difficult for me to just sit back and allow it. It was tradition here for the man to arrange it, and despite my desire to help, I really had no idea what needed to be done, so I guess I was receiving another lesson in letting go of control.

It was decided our marriage would take place in Pokhara at the Temple Bidhya basini, nearby to where Govin and I had been living. Govin said this would be best, otherwise we would have to invite the whole of Baglung and that would be expensive. Part of me was disappointed, as I would have loved to have experienced the whole of Baglung celebrating. What an experience that would have been. Nonetheless, I could see the practicality of his suggestion. This way it was a bit secret, and he could save face in the community for not inviting them all.

We had around seventy to eighty guests and it was in full Nepali/Hindu style. My new friend Martha was my chosen bridesmaid, as none of my family could be there, and we elected her mother and aunties to be my family for the day. They were truly an amazing bunch of women. Coming from a higher caste, Govin was so nervous that they would judge him, but they were truly lovely. They took care of me the night before the marriage, preparing a feast with dancing, and I stayed the night to prepare for the big day. It was a lovely experience spending time with these women and learning about their marriage customs.

The next morning, it was not much different to any other wedding for a bride to be, makeup, hair, everyone fussing, then eventually I was ready. Wearing all red and a little gold to break it up was so strange for me, but here in Nepal, these are the traditional colours for a wedding, not white. Red is the symbolism of purity, honour and dignity.

Upon arrival with my entourage of pretend family behind me, I was overwhelmed and suddenly aware of my nerves. I never thought I would do this again, especially in another culture, yet here I was. My love for Govin was never in question. To sign the paperwork months before for the government registration of our marriage was easy. It was just paperwork. But now here we were declaring our union not only in front of family and friends but in front of God Shiva in his temple. I was feeling a little like a phoney being there. Although as soon as I walked up the many steps in my dainty little red shoes and saw him, I knew it was right. I never felt more beautiful in my life, more loved and protected. Here was this man, who had nothing, and yet I felt more love, support, protection, and security with him than I had ever felt. I felt vulnerable, but safe. Such strange new feelings.

The ceremony took place in the smallest little temple. I could not help but imagine my family trying to fit inside there with me. It would have been impossible. At best, it was big enough for three people, yet somehow, we had at least five people and another four to six heads peering through the doorway. In the temple, surrounded by our close family and friends, sharing Tikka, rings, garlands and a beautiful necklace, I also had to participate in dhog, which is putting my head to his feet and spilling water around him in a circle three times as part of the union.

It was interesting to me, but I actually felt honoured to participate in the dhog (touching Govin's feet) – haha he has beautiful feet. Okay, I have a strange foot fetish, but that aside, the idea of showing him my devotion and commitment by touching his feet with my forehead was the least I could do. He was, in that moment, my king, my god, as I was his goddess and queen. For me, it was the symbolic gesture of the feminine and masculine joined to accomplish great things together. Finally, I had found what union meant; it was a far cry from the marriage I had experienced at twenty, with my fairy tale ideals. This one felt very different, grounded, balanced and on purpose. This one felt rooted in traditions that were over 6,000 years old, and for some reason, I felt the gods were smiling down over us.

Not long after celebrating our union, Govin's family lost their uncle to alcoholism, sadly a common problem in Nepali communities. He was the brother to Sanu Ama and to Govin, a special uncle, as he went to his village multiple times in his childhood. He enjoyed working on the farm and escaping his hard life in Baglung.

Nepali funerals are very different from anything I have ever experienced, a far cry from the church style, sombre ceremonies that I have often witnessed here in Australia. Within hours of the death, the nearest family members take the body and wash it, purifying it and wrapping it in white cloth. Then they trek the body down the mountains to the Kali Gandaki River. All the mourners gather round, and the body is burned on a pile of wood on the riverside. Once all is done, the ashes and remains end up in the river, washed away. It is amazing how fast they get this done.

The sons shave their heads, bathe and wear white cloth, the daughters also bathe and wrap themselves in sombre saris. They then retreat to the home of the father, and the family gather to support them.

We arrived at the family home high in the mountain late in the afternoon the next day and were greeted with smiles. For me, this was such a strange experience. Everyone came to stay and sleep nearby and support the immediate family. The wife was crying, however, I mostly witnessed the family sitting in quiet contemplation, breaking this occasionally with light conversation and even a little laughter. I felt like I was a welcome distraction.

In the home, they had cleaned it all out. They were to spend the next thirteen days sleeping on straw on the floor, only eating rice once or twice a day with no salt, no dairy or meat products allowed. Black tea was also allowed. Whilst they honour their dead this way, there were also rules about not touching the grieving family and we were not allowed to touch the walls and certain areas of the home that had been purified.

I tried to become a little invisible and hid away in the straw at the side of the home, rugged up against the cold reading my book. Despite the circumstances, this place was a beautiful, peaceful place, and I appreciated just being there to witness this intimate family event. The next day we woke up and Govin took me walking through the rice fields to his cousin's home. It's always a pleasure walking in Nepal. Apart from bike riding, there truly is no better way to explore this amazing countryside with views in any direction. When we left, Govin made a joke, 'I bet you could not do this'.

'What?' I asked.

'Sit at home for thirteen days with nothing to do, eating rice and tea after I am dead.'

I laughed; he knew me too well. But I'd damn well rise to the challenge.

Chapter 30
Bistaari. Bistaari, Just Breathe

There was so much anticipation and excitement in the wait for my cousin and her family to arrive from Australia. After nine months in Nepal, I was ready to be a tourist with them. Govin and I had arranged to take them to Jomsom and Muktinath trekking. A first for us all.

Feeling reasonably fit and healthy after much walking due to the petrol crisis – and life in Nepal requires walking for many reasons – I was eager to get out into nature again and walk in the mountains.

Driving up to Jomsom in the Jeep took us around ten hours. Typically, driving anywhere in Nepal takes time, but this was a challenging route because of the 4WD goat tracks, or should I say yak tracks, which formed a good part of the journey, with drops on the side of the road that were literally straight down into the raging Kali Gandaki. Driving in Nepal is an experience which I adore for some strange reason. From Kathmandu to Pokhara, some 200 kilometres apart, takes buses around seven to eight hours. The ride is almost always filled with adventure and, let's say, roadblocks of some sort, so that on any journey in Nepal it's best to be okay with not being in a hurry.

After the occasional seat exchange to prevent car sickness and a flat tyre about seven kilometres out of Jomsom where we danced and chatted excitedly to keep warm in the zero temperatures in the early evening, we eventually arrived and were ready to eat and get our legs back on solid ground.

The next morning, we woke early and managed to find cappuccinos (Wow! A real treat in these parts), and after breakfast, started our trek out of Jomsom. Trying to describe the terrain and environment here is almost impossible; a winding valley between some of the highest white peaks in the world, appearing so close that you felt you could reach out and touch them, yet they were definitely out of reach for amateur hikers like us.

The valley we walked through was the amazing Kali Gandaki riverbed that in the monsoon flows fast and brings the water down the mountains. Now it was the dry winter season, so the riverbed was a huge expanse of black pebbles and rocks that in parts were easily three kms wide. The lower terrain reminded me of films I'd seen showing the landscape on the moon or Mars; a desert or barren land with the occasional shrub, not much can grow out there. The weather was a series of extremes. Anything living out there must be resilient, tolerant, patient and extremely hardy people, animals, or plants. As we walked further into the Lower Mustang region, the animals, plants, and people seemed to get smaller. Houses changed and looked more Tibetan in their appearance than Nepali. The people also looked more Tibetan, and their spirituality was a mixture of Hindu and Buddhism. The language according to Govin was slower, drawn out Nepali. He giggled often at the way they spoke to him. Being there was like being in another country, only about 250 kilometres from Pokhara.

After we walked approximately fifteen kilometres, mostly on the flats and riverbed, we reached Kagbeni, a cute little village just at the bottom of the ascent to Muktinath. Feeling optimistic and ravenously hungry, we had a great lunch at a typical Mustang lodge and prepared ourselves for the second half of the day. As soon as we left Kagbeni with our Momo and Dhal Bhat filled bellies, I noticed the air getting thinner. The way out of the village was a steep accent, and it slowed our pace considerably. Having no choice, we adjusted to the lack of oxygen available at this altitude. We slowly walked the winding uphill trail, and we seemed to venture into more barren land. Thinking we only had two hours left of walking, we stayed optimistic, resting regularly to regain our breath.

Five hours later, we were still walking. OMG, at this altitude we were stopping every ten steps and breathing so heavily, starting to feel dizzy and our legs were exhausted. It seemed the lack of oxygen had fatigued the whole body. It was now dark and using the moonlight, we slowly walked the last four hundred metres, taking us about forty minutes instead of fifteen minutes. We were exhausted, flopping ourselves through the doorway of the first guest house in Muktinath, and slowly regained our breath. It was funny to me how the altitude can affect so many things; my appetite was non-existent, my head felt dizzy, and I felt slightly nauseated.

Forcing some food down, I went to sleep with the thought that maybe I wouldn't wake up. Apparently, that can happen here to some people, however I was so tired at this point I wasn't fazed by the thought, and it seemed nobody else was either.

In the morning, we woke early to the most spectacular view. Honestly, it was something pictures could not capture. The feeling of being surrounded by snow-capped peaks that seemed to touch the sky, with air so fresh and crisp, dressed in layers of yak woollies and sipping warm tea, it was like being in heaven. The temple was still another twenty-minute walk up the hill and Govin got up early to go and pray like a good Hindu, and then he took us again after breakfast. We ascended with him guiding us up the many steps past the bells and prayer wheels, following the winding stream that rushed past us down the mountain, no doubt to meet up with Kali Gandaki somewhere down below. The air was still really thin and despite the good night's sleep; it was apparent that we still needed to move very slowly up here. Interestingly, it did not seem to affect Govin at all, he had already been up twice to the temple which sat 3,800 metres above sea level. Once again 'bistaari bistaari'.

The Muktinath, Shiva temple is a significant temple in Nepal, with millions of Hindus and Buddhists making the sacred pilgrimage to the temple every year to cleanse themselves in the purest water in the Himalayas. They also came to witness the never-ending fire that has been continuously burning for thousands of years due to the natural gas that runs underground in this area, whilst receiving blessings from their beloved Shiva. Hindus call the temple Mukti Kshetra, which literally means the 'place of salvation' at the foot of the Thorong La Mountain pass, Mustang, Nepal. Govin was very excited and happy to make this pilgrimage with us, as he had never been before. He shared with me it was really special to him and that he wished to bring his family there one day, especially his mother.

One thing that I felt as I reached the temple was silence, except for the sounds of nature and rushing water. It was a strange silence. It was like there was a presence watching over us, an energy holding us, like you could just be. I am not sure if it was the running water or the amazing views, but a deep emotion came over me of connection and realisation of oneness. It took me by surprise as I stood on the step and just breathed it in and allowed myself to shed a tear. Maybe it was the altitude, but I felt like no matter what was ahead of me in my life, that I was being held and guided... I felt gratitude for the breath of life.

The temple was not that different from any other in Nepal. It isn't even that grand to look at, but the position it commands is nothing short of breathtaking. Honestly, it was awe-inspiring to stand and look out from the temple at the landscape falling away from you and the white mountain peaks in all directions. The Hindus come here and pray, but before they do, they remove their clothes and run through the coldest water fountains, all 108 of them, to cleanse themselves and remove impurities under the watchful eye of Shiva, the mountain God.

The number 108 carries great significance in Eastern philosophy. In Hindu astrology, there are twelve zodiac or Rashi and nine planets or Graha, giving a total of 108 combinations. They often suggest that there are 108 paths to God and in Ayurveda, there are 108 marmas, pressure points in the body which all converge at the heart.

Watching a group of young men stripping down to their underwear and doing exactly this was so exhilarating that I wanted to join them. However, I was mindful and somewhat conveniently confused about whether I'd be being disrespectful, so watched instead and then after they were finished, I ran my hand under every fountain. Splashing the icy water all over my head, arms and chest was so refreshing and revitalising it reminded me of swimming off the Bass Coast in Australia near my home on Phillip Island. The feeling of immersing yourself in cold water really has a cleansing and revitalising effect, and it made me think of home and how much I missed my island. Later, I learned that in the early hours of that morning, Govin had gone up to the temple to take part in the ritual praying for our future and for his family.

After spending some time at the temple, we descended, and I immediately felt invigorated and ready for the day ahead. We now had to head back down the mountain to Jomsom and continue walking back along the Kali Gandaki River towards Beni. This would take us the next four days.

So, with each step, I felt a bounce and was almost dancing down the mountain toward Jomsom. I felt assured, and my feet just seemed to find the path, which was strange for me as I had dodgy knees, so my usual habit would be to nurse my knees down a mountain such as this. However, something had changed. I felt like I was twenty-eight again, flying free and my body felt light. We walked through mountain villages and so much of our walking was done in deep thought and meditation. The landscape slowly changed, and the views continuously inspired us as we walked over and through and around the trails, following Kali down to Marpha.

Marpha was an intriguing village. It was famous for its apples, which by now I was familiar with as Govin would cheekily ask farmers to throw us one from the field as we walked past all the apple farms along the trek.

Marpha was about all things apples. It was the kind of village with nooks and crannies everywhere, the kind of place that you would want to explore for a few days, with a beautiful Buddhist Monastery that sat high above the village. People here had built their homes into the land with stone and their roofs served as storage spaces for wood and other household needs, including washing. Their animals had their own little walled yards protected from the weather, too. The whole village was a labyrinth of stone paths, stone walls, and intriguing doorways. The next day, we headed further south to the village of Kalopani.

By the time we reached Kalopani on our fifth day of trekking, after many freezing nights and fresh days, I was ready to board the bus, my knees becoming aware of their lack of cartilage. The local bus was packed to the roof, literally, with bags and people. Nepali take advantage of every available space and for the next three hours to Beni, we bounced around on the 4WD track down along the edge of cliffs not more than three metres wide in places on a bus with babies and old people all hanging on to whatever they could reach. At least ten people sat on the bags in the aisles, leaning on each other to support themselves. Despite the crammed in feeling, I loved every minute; this was daily life for many Nepali in this region. I learnt my biggest lessons on trust during this adventure.

Arriving back in Pokhara later that evening, I felt a soft sadness, at the realisation I only had twelve days left in this country of temples, gods and crazy bus rides, and most of all, I would be leaving the most amazing man that I had ever met. Australian immigration doesn't appreciate human smuggling, so we would have to be patient and do all the paperwork necessary for Govin to join me in Australia. I was full of mixed emotions, the excitement of coming home to my family, friends, and my island, to the grief of leaving a place that had literally changed my life and perceptions about my life.

So much had happened in such a short time, yet it felt like an entire lifetime, and I learnt so much. Another chapter of life written and done, and all I could do now was to reflect on the past and focus on the future and writing the next chapter of my life. I was excited to go home and share what I'd experienced. I was looking forward to reconnecting with my work, supporting and inspiring people to follow their dreams, to not be afraid, and to have courage. To know that sometimes following your heart can bring challenges, however, the challenges far out way the suffering of feeling powerless and stuck in a life that does not fit who you are. Challenges are just opportunities to shift your perceptions. Sometimes we think we know and as soon as we think this, you can be assured the universe will remind you that you don't know anything at all.

Last Chapter 31
My Mother-In-Law Once Said To Me, 'Do they Have a Moon in Australia?'

To have vision is to have clarification, to perceive and know without a doubt. To be clear-sighted about the way forward. To be visionary.

A visionary can see the 'whole' picture with absolute clarity. A visionary knows exactly where they are headed and knows that as long as they stay focused, they will get to their destination. They do not see positive and negative as separate things, they recognise the totality of everything and that all have purpose, they see truth.

A visionary does not always know the exact route and way to the destination, they are realists and know that there will always be learning and challenges connected to their vision. There will be sacrifices. They know this is necessary to fully reap the rewards of achieving this vision. This means they have to walk the whole pilgrimage, otherwise they cannot get the wisdom of the journey. Ultimately, this is the reason for any journey.

A visionary will allow themselves to stay in tune, connected to the source, to be guided by their heart centre. They know, without a doubt, as long as they stay focused on the 'vision' that they will be gently guided toward that vision in divine timing. A visionary accepts that along the way they may have to go through dark forests, slay dragons and at times become disorientated, scared, overwhelmed and momentarily lost.

A visionary knows that all the events that occur along the way are necessary, as to arrive at the destination without the tools he gathers along the way is to arrive too early and ill prepared. Thus, the vision may dissipate and not last, like a mirage in the desert. A visionary has patience and accepts the journey as an opportunity to grow and learn.

The day came when it was finally time for me to head home. We had been working on Govin's visa the whole time, and as anyone who has been on that road knows, bureaucracy around visas is like being in a dark hole with no flashlight. We decided it would be best if I headed home to work on the visa and start to prepare things in Australia for him to come. My family also needed to reconnect, and I could feel this strongly. I really did not want to leave him. He had become such a massive part of my life in such a short time. But we had spent every day together, we knew each other and felt we could handle the distance.

The reality of leaving him that day was unbelievably hard. I think I cried almost the entire way home to Australia; I'm certain people must have thought someone had died. For me, it was like a part of me had been taken. I was missing my right arm, or was it my left?

This man had showed me more courage, more love and emotional support just by showing up and being himself than I had ever experienced from a man. I was excited, and also a little scared, of course, for our future. But I was certain we were meant to be sharing and witnessing each other's journeys. It was not that we did not have our differences, of course, culturally there are many. However, the willingness in which he embraced and wanted to learn about me and me about him, I felt assured that together we could create a solid partnership. A partnership that would forever be evolving, changing, and accepting.

Along the journey home, I imagined all the possibilities of our life in Australia, and I found it helped to focus on the possibilities instead of the losses. By the time I arrived in Melbourne twentyfive hours later, I was determined to create a new way of living in the world.

After my time away, I learnt so much about connection, about contribution and creation. I equally learnt about destruction and disconnection. I learnt about being, space, and timing. I realised my potential and let go of my limitations. I started to believe in myself; I believed I could make a difference in people's lives, and it was becoming clearer how.

I wanted to create a tribe, a community of like-minded people who wanted to make their career or life about giving, inspiring, empowering and lifting people up to their potential; to follow their dharma.

Through writing this book and unlocking so many of the lessons I had received, I have concluded that I am as ready as I will ever be to step up and contribute to something greater. I have rid myself of nearly all my possessions, debts and ties and now I am simply me. I feel free to be able to create as I have made space to do so. No longer am I bound to direct debits, house payments and credit cards. Now I am living to create, not merely survive. I am excited about the present, even more excited about the future, and the past is simply a series of experiences that shaped me to be where I am, forever grateful.

As I arrived home to Australia, I decided to sell my house. As usual, the universe always wants to throw that curve ball to check if you mean what you say, so of course this did not go to plan. The settlement was delayed, and as my money was now officially all gone, I was back to that place I had been many times before in my life of having no money. Of course, my ego went into meltdown and I started getting frantic about not having money, being catapulted back into that very Australian energy of doing security and money. For a short time, I turned my attention to a temporary job whilst I was waiting for my 'real' job to be ready. As a contractor for Bounce, it meant the next teaching course for me to run would not be until February. It was December.

Not only that, at the same time I was being bombarded by the needs of my children, and before long I was being pulled into their energy and that of friends, too. After nearly a year of being connected to me, within a swift moment, I was disconnected again from me, from my vision and the planet. I had fallen back into survival mode.

A friend helped with accommodation, and I took a job locally at Phillip Island, thinking, 'yeah I can do this, it's all good, it's just for the summer'. Within days of taking this job, the heaviness feeling came back, that feeling of hopelessness and a feeling of deep disconnection, like I had stepped off the yellow brick road.

I went to the beach and meditated on this feeling and within minutes, I realised I was off path again. The universe needed me to focus on my vision. It needed me to have faith. All the things that Nepal had taught me were still there, I just needed to use them. I was reminded of the perfection in everything, that in this imperfect situation, there was actually perfection. I vowed to take this time to write my book.

I managed to get some funds from the purchaser of my house and once again started having faith in my ability to co-create my life. I found my connection, and the feeling came rushing back. The momentum followed, the networks followed, and before long, I was back on track. My vision for 'the reconnection tribe' had returned bigger and better than ever. I am back in the flow. What happens next? Well, you will have to wait for book number two.

It seems my love affair with Nepal had become more than just the love of a country. It became the place where I learnt to follow my dharma.

The next chapter we faced as a married couple, a united energy, was the visa journey to Australia. I could not wait to show Govin my part of the world as he had shown me his. Life is funny though, as soon as you think you know, you can be assured you know nothing.

Coming home for me was a feeling, not a place. I have many places in the world that are home for me and always, always, they are places that invoke a feeling. Home is a feeling. Home is love. Feeling settled in love, grounded and connected in love; this was a first for me, Following my Dharma.

After sixteen months of long distance FaceTime chats and long phone calls, I returned to Nepal in January 2017. After unexpected back surgery and not seeing Govin for over six months, I had decided that I would not leave him until his visa arrived. Two months later, at the end of March, we got that amazing email, and in disbelief, the wait was over. Govin stepped foot on Aussie soil on 1 April 2017.

Through learning and accepting our Values and Core Beliefs, we can become more aligned with our Dharma – our Purpose – and we can start to live more meaningful lives, consciously, connected, creatively and with contribution.

More great Shawline titles can be found by scanning the QR code below. New titles also available through Books@Home Pty Ltd.
Subscribe today at www.booksathome.com.au or scan the QR code below.

www.ingramcontent.com/pod-product-compliance
Lightning Source LLC
Chambersburg PA
CBHW011445130526
44590CB00065B/3873